Hibernate, Spring & Struts

Interview Questions

You'll Most Likely Be Asked

Job Interview Questions Series

www.vibrantpublishers.com

Hibernate, Spring & Struts Interview Questions You'll Most Likely Be Asked

ISBN-10: 1456518380
ISBN-13: 978-14-56518-38-7

Library of Congress Control Number: 2011920203

The publisher wishes to thank Dana Mitrea (Romania) for her invaluable inputs to this edition.

Here's what others say about this book!

I have many Job Interview Question Series books from Vibrant Publishers - Java, .NET, etc. These book don't let you down. I referred it again and again and again. It is amazing! - *Jacob Churchill*

Great book for students as well as professionals! - *Narayan Shastri*

The layout of the book is good and so is the Index. A great complete package. - *Cherry David*

The book has plenty of useful information. Serious "must have" for all job seekers and job hoppers. - *Jane*

Great layout, superb coverage of topics and just enough info to prepare you for your D day. Absolute buy for every job seeker. - *G. Thomas*

This page is intentionally left blank

Hibernate, Spring & Struts Questions

Review these typical interview questions and think about how you would answer them. Read the answers listed; you will find best possible answers along with strategies and suggestions.

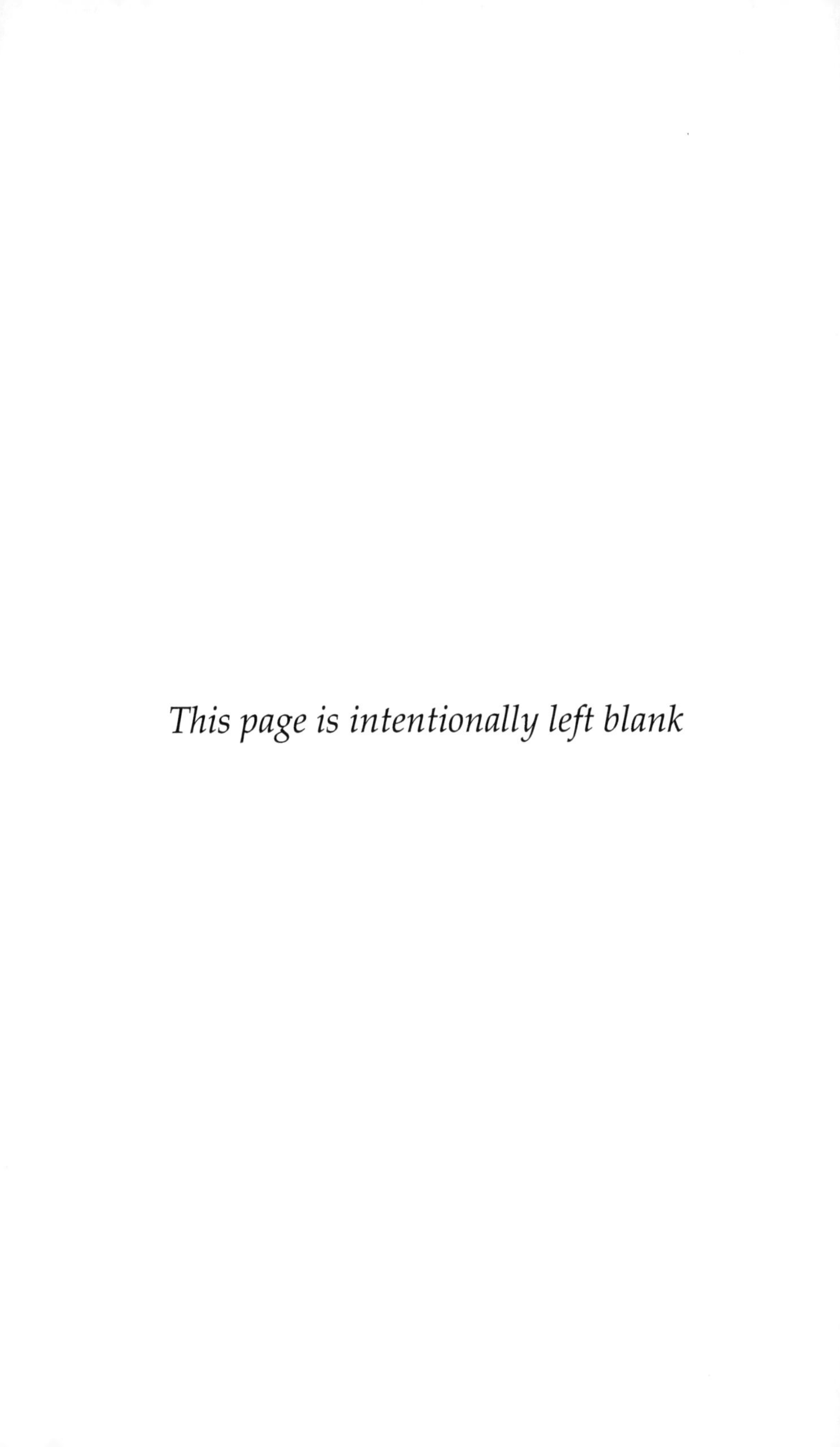
This page is intentionally left blank

Hibernate

1: Define the persistence concept.

Answer:

Persistence is a fundamental concept in application development which allows an object to outlive the process that created it. The state of the object can be stored to disk, and an object with the same state can be re-created at some point in the future.

2: What is ORM?

Answer:

Object/relational mapping is automated (and transparent) persistence of objects in a Java application to the tables in a relational database; it uses metadata that describes the mapping between the objects and the database.

3: Which are the main components of an ORM solution?

Answer:

An ORM solution consists of the following four components:

a) an API for performing basic CRUD operations on objects of persistent classes

b) a language or API for specifying queries that refer to classes and properties of classes

c) a facility for specifying mapping metadata

d) A technique for the ORM implementation to interact with transactional objects to perform dirty checking, lazy association fetching, and other optimization functions.

4: Which are the four levels of ORM quality?

Answer:

a) *Pure relational* - the whole application, including the user interface, is designed around the relational model and SQL-based relational operations

b) *Light object mapping* - entities are represented as classes that are mapped manually to the relational tables.

c) *Medium object mapping* - the application is designed around an object model; SQL is generated at build time using a code-generation tool, or at runtime by framework code.

d) *Full object mapping* - supports sophisticated object modeling: composition, inheritance, polymorphism, and persistence by reachability.

5: What is Hibernate?

Answer:

Hibernate is a solution for object relational mapping and a persistence management solution or persistent layer. It provides all the ORM benefits: productivity, maintainability, performance, vendor independence.

6: What is the Hibernate Core?

Answer:

It is the base service for persistence, with its native API and its mapping metadata stored in XML files. It has a query language called HQL (almost the same as SQL), as well as programmatic query interfaces for Criteria and Example queries.

7: What is a Hibernate Session?

Answer:

It is a single-threaded nonshared object that represents a particular unit of work with the database. It contains the persistence manager API which can be called to load and store objects.

8: Give several reasons for using a database connection pool.

Answer:

a) Acquiring a new connection is expensive; some database management systems even start a completely new server process for each connection.

b) Maintaining many idle connections is expensive for a database management system, and the pool can optimize the usage of idle connections (or disconnect if there are no requests).

c) Creating prepared statements is also expensive for some drivers, and the connection pool can cache statements for a connection across requests

9: What is Hibernate EntityManager?

Answer:

Hibernate EntityManager is a wrapper around Hibernate Core that provides the JPA programming interfaces, supports the JPA entity instance lifecycle, and allows the developer to write queries with the standardized Java Persistence query language.

10: What is a persistence-unit?

Answer:

A persistence-unit can be seen as the configuration of an EMF together with a set of mapping metadata (usually annotated classes). EMF comes from EntityManagerFactory and represents an interface used by the application to obtain an application-managed entity manager.

11: What is Java Transaction API?

Answer:

Java Transaction API (JTA) is the standardized service interface for transaction control in Java enterprise applications. It exposes several interfaces, such as the UserTransaction API for transaction demarcation and the TransactionManager API for participation in the transaction lifecycle.

12: Which are the main components of Hibernate architecture?

Answer:

a) *Connection management* - provides efficient management of the database connections.

b) *Transaction management* - provides the ability to the user to execute more than one database statements at a time.

c) *Object relational mapping* - a technique of mapping the data representation from an object model to a relational data model

13: How does Hibernate handle persistent associations?

Answer:

Hibernate doesn't manage persistent associations. If somebody wants to manipulate an association, one must write exactly the same code he/she would write without Hibernate. If an association is bidirectional, both sides of the relationship must be considered.

14: What is the purpose of JTATransactionFactory?

Answer:

It is a factory class for JTATransaction instances. It does several things:

a) Enables correct Session scoping and propagation for JTA if somebody decides to use the SessionFactory.getCurrentSession() method instead of opening and closing every Session manually.

b) Tells Hibernate that the developer is planning to call the JTA UserTransaction interface in the application to start, commit, or roll back system transactions.

c) switches the Hibernate Transaction API to JTA, in case somebody doesn't want to work with the standardized UserTransaction

15: What is the purpose of the object/relational mapping metadata?

Answer:

Metadata is data about data, and mapping metadata defines and governs the transformation between the different type systems and relationship representations in object-oriented and SQL systems. It specifies the mapping between classes and tables, properties and columns, associations and foreign keys, Java types and SQL types, and so on.

16: What does the following code snippet?

```
package hibernate.test;
import javax.persistence.*;
@Entity
@Table(name = "TEST")
public class Test {
}
```

Answer:

It declares class Test as a persistent entity. All of its properties are now automatically persistent with a default strategy. The second annotation declares the name of the table in the database schema.

17: What are the benefits of using annotations?

Answer:

One of the clear benefits of using annotations is that they offer flexibility for agile development. Most development tools and editors can't refactor XML element and attribute values/ but annotations are part of the Java language and are included in all refactoring operations.

18: Which Java library contains support for annotations?

Answer:

Annotations from the Java Persistence are available in javax.persistence package. One can use these annotations to declare persistent entity classes, embeddable classes, properties, fields, keys, and so on.

19: Which notion has brought XDoclet project?

Answer:

The XDoclet project has brought the notion of attribute-oriented programming to Java. XDoclet leverages the Javadoc tag format (@attribute) to specify class-, field-, or method-level metadata attributes.

20: Provide an example of an entity placeholder.

Answer:

```
<?xml version="1.0"?>
[
 <!ENTITY idgenerator "auction.custom.MyOracleGenerator">
]>

<id name="id" column="CATEGORY_ID" type="long">
 <generator class="&idgenerator;"/>
</id>
```

The &idgenerator; value is called an entity placeholder. The XML parser will substitute it on Hibernate startup, when mapping files are read.

21: Which are the built-in entity modes in Hibernate?

Answer:

Hibernate has three built-in entity modes:

a) *POJO* — a domain model implementation based on POJOs, persistent classes.

b) *MAP* — no Java classes are required; entities are represented in the Java application with HashMaps. This mode allows quick prototyping of fully dynamic applications.

c) *DOM4J* — no Java classes are required; entities are represented as XML elements, based on the dom4j API. This mode is especially useful for exporting or importing data, or for rendering and transforming data through XSLT processing.

22: What is the distinction made by Hibernate between objects of entity type and objects of value type?

Answer:

The objects of entity type have their own database identity (primary key value) while the objects of value type have no database identity - they belong to an entity instance and their persistent state is embedded in the table row of the owning entity.

23: What are the things that need to be taken into account when implementing POJOs from the domain model diagram?

Answer:

The three things that need to taken into account are the following:

a) *Shared references* – POJO classes must be written in a way that avoids shared references to value type instances.

b) *Lifecycle dependencies*– the lifecycle of a value-type instance is bound to that of its owning entity instance; the application workflow and user interface must be designed to respect and expect lifecycle dependencies.

c) *Identity* – entity classes need an identifier property in almost all cases. User defined value-type classes (and JDK classes) don't have an identifier property/ because instances are identified through the owning entity.

24: How does Hibernate expose database identity to the application?

Answer:

Hibernate exposes this info in two ways:

a) through the value of the identifier property of a persistent instance

b) through the value returned by Session.getIdentifier (Object entity)

25: Provide an example of mapping a regular (noncomposite) identifier property in Hibernate XML files.

Answer:

```
<class name="Category" table="CATEGORY">
 <id name="id" column="CATEGORY_ID" type="long">
  <generator class="native"/>
```

</id>

</class>

26: Which properties need to satisfy a candidate key in order to become a primary key?

Answer:

A candidate key must satisfy the following conditions:

a) Its value (for any column of the candidate key) is never null.

b) Each row has a unique value.

c) The value of a particular row never changes

27: What is a natural key?

Answer:

A natural key is a key with business meaning: an attribute or combination of attributes that is unique by virtue of its business semantics. Examples of natural keys are the U.S. Social Security Number or Australian Tax File Number. Distinguishing natural keys is simple: If a candidate key attribute has meaning outside the database context/ it's a natural key, whether or not it's automatically generated.

28: What are the attributes of a good primary key?

Answer:

A good primary key must be unique, constant, and required (never null or unknown). Few entity attributes satisfy these requirements/ and some that do can't be efficiently indexed by SQL databases (although this is an implementation detail and shouldn't be the primary motivation for or against a particular key).

29: Give example of several Hibernate built-in identifier generators.

Answer:

a) *Native* - used in order to keep the mapping metadata portable to different database management systems

b) *Identity* - supports identity columns in DB2, MySQL, MS SQL Server, Sybase, and HypersonicSQL. The returned identifier is of type long, short, or int.

c) *Sequence* - creates a sequence in DB2, PostgreSQL, Oracle, SAP DB and so on

d) *Increment* - reads the maximum (numeric) primary key column value of the table and increments the value by one each time a new row is inserted; it is especially efficient if the single-server Hibernate application has exclusive access to the database but should not be used in any other scenario.

e) *Hilo* - generates identifiers that are unique only for a particular database. High values are retrieved from a global source and are made unique by adding a local low value.

f) *Seqhilo* - works like the regular hilo generator, except it uses a named database sequence to generate high values.

g) *uuid.hex* - 128-bit UUID generator (an algorithm that generates identifiers of type string, unique within a network, based on IP address used in combination with a unique timestamp)

h) *Guid* - provides a database-generated globally unique identifier string on MySQL and SQL Server.

i) *Select* - retrieves a primary key assigned by a database trigger by selecting the row by some unique key and retrieving the primary key value.

30: What is the purpose of dynamic-insert and dynamic-update attributes?

Answer:

The dynamic-insert attribute tells Hibernate whether to include null property values in an SQL INSERT, and the dynamic-update attribute tells Hibernate whether to include unmodified properties in the SQL UPDATE.

31: What is an immutable POJO? Give example of mapping an immutable entity using annotations.

Answer:

A POJO is immutable if no public setter methods for any properties of the class are exposed—all values are set in the constructor. Usage example:

```
@Entity
@org.hibernate.annotations.Entity(mutable = false)
@org.hibernate.annotations.AccessType("field")
public class Test { ...
}
```

32: Describe the interface NamingStrategy.

Answer:

It consists of a set of rules for determining the physical column and table names given the information in the mapping document. The interface may be used to implement project-scoped naming standards for database objects.

33: Describe the dynamic behavior offered by NamingStrategy interface.

Answer:

In order to activate a specific naming strategy, one can pass an instance to the Hibernate Configuration at startup:

```
Configuration cfg = new Configuration();
cfg.setNamingStrategy( new CENamingStrategy() );
SessionFactory sessionFactory sf = cfg.configure().buildSessionFactory();
```

This allows having multiple SessionFactory instances based on the same mapping documents, each using a different NamingStrategy. This is extremely useful in a multiclient installation, where unique table names (but the same data model) are required for each client.

34: What feature does Hibernate use in order to determine the Java type of the property?

Answer:

Reflection - The process by which a computer program can observe and modify its own structure and behavior at runtime.

35: Describe the rules applied when a property of a persistent class is not annotated.

Answer:

a) If the property is of a JDK type/ it's automatically persistent.

b) If the class of the property is annotated as @Embeddable/ it's mapped as a component of the owning class.

c) If the type of the property is Serializable, its value is stored in its serialized form.

36: What is the purpose of @Basic annotation?

Answer:

The @Basic annotation marks the property as not optional on the Java object level.

37: Which attribute is used in XML mapping files in order to control the default access strategy for a class?

Answer:

Default-access attribute of the hibernate-mapping root element. It may have the following values: field, property, noop, custom.Class.

38: Describe several approaches to representing an inheritance hierarchy.

Answer:

There are four different approaches to representing an inheritance hierarchy:

a) *Table per concrete class with implicit polymorphism* – no explicit inheritance mapping is used, and default runtime polymorphic behavior.

b) *Table per concrete class* – discard polymorphism and inheritance relationships completely from the SQL schema.

c) *Table per class hierarchy* – enable polymorphism by denormalizing the SQL schema, and utilize a type discriminator column that holds type information.

d) *Table per subclass* – represent is a (inheritance) relationship and has a (foreign key) relationships.

39: Which Hibernate element can be used in order to create a table per class hierarchy mapping?

Answer:

The <subclass> element. For example:

```
<hibernate-mapping>
 <class name="BillingDetails" table="BILLING_DETAILS">
  <id name="id" column="BILLING_DETAILS_ID" type="long">
   <generator class="native"/>
  </id>
 ...
 <subclass name="CreditCard" discriminator-value="CC">
  <property name="number" column="CC_NUMBER"/>
  <property name="expMonth" column="CC_EXP_MONTH"/>
  <property name="expYear" column="CC_EXP_YEAR"/>
 </subclass>
 ...
 </class>
</hibernate-mapping>
```

40: Which Hibernate element can be used in order to create a table per subclass mapping?

Answer:

The <joined-subclass> element. Example:

```
<hibernate-mapping>
 <class name="BillingDetails" table="BILLING_DETAILS">
  <id name="id" column="BILLING_DETAILS_ID" type="long">
   <generator class="native"/>
  </id>
  ...
  <joined-subclass name="CreditCard" table="CREDIT_CARD">
   <key column="CREDIT_CARD_ID"/>
   <property name="number" column="NUMBER"/>
   <property name="expMonth" column="EXP_MONTH"/>
   <property name="expYear" column="EXP_YEAR"/>
  </joined-subclass>

  ...
 </class>
</hibernate-mapping>
```

41: Is it possible to apply the mapping strategies to abstract classes and interfaces?

Answer:

Yes. Interfaces may have no state but may contain accessor method declarations, so they can be treated like abstract classes. An interface can be mapped with <class>, <union-subclass>, <subclass>, or <joined-subclass>. Hibernate won't try to instantiate an abstract class, even if one queries or loads it.

42: What are the interfaces provided by Hibernate that applications may use when defining custom mapping types?

Answer:

These interfaces, known as extension points, reduce the work involved in creating new mapping types and insulate the custom type from changes to the Hibernate core. Hibernate's extension points are as follows:

a) *UserType* — the basic extension point, which provides the basic methods for custom loading and storing of value type instances.

b) *CompositeUserType* — an interface with more methods than the basic UserType, used to expose internals about the value type class to Hibernate, such as the individual properties.

c) *UserCollectionType* — rarely needed interface that is used to implement custom collections.

d) *EnhancedUserType* — an interface that extends UserType and provides additional methods for marshalling value types to and from XML representations.

e) *UserVersionType* — an interface that extends UserType and provides additional methods enabling the custom mapping type for usage in entity version mappings.

f) *ParameterizedType* — a useful interface that can be combined with all others to provide configuration settings—that is, parameters defined in metadata.

43: Which Java collections are supported by Hibernate?

Answer:

Set, SortedSet, List, Collection, Map, SortedMap, Arrays.

44: What is the effect of cascade on inverse?

Answer:

If somebody decides to cascade operations from one side of an entity relationship to associated entities, he/she saves the lines of code needed to manage the state of the other side manually - that object state becomes transitive. Cascade and inverse have in common the fact that they don't appear on collections of value types or on any other value-type mappings. The rules for these are implied by the nature of value types.

45: What is a many-valued entity association?

Answer:

It is a collection of entity references. There are two types of many-valued entity associations: one-to-many and many-to-many.

46: What is a polymorphic association?

Answer:

A polymorphic association is an association that may refer instances of a subclass of the class that was explicitly specified in the mapping metadata.

47: Which operations have Hibernate to handle in order to support portability across different DBMS?

Answer:

To support this portability, Hibernate has to handle three kinds of operations:

a) every data-retrieval operation results in SELECT statements being executed.

b) every data modification requires the execution of Data Manipulation Language (DML) statements, such as UPDATE, INSERT, and DELETE.

c) a database schema must be created or altered before DML and data retrieval can be executed.

48: Which are the rules that ensure data consistency?

Answer:

There are four levels of rules that protect the information and guarantee that it's never in an inconsistent state0

a) *domain constraint* – defines the range of possible values a particular datatype can handle

b) *column constraint* – restricting a column to hold values of a particular domain is equivalent to adding a column constraint

c) *table constraint* – an integrity rule that applies to a single row or several rows is a table constraint

d) *database constraint* – if a rule applies to more than one table, it has database scope

49: What support does Hibernate offer for index creation?

Answer:

In Hibernate, indexes can be created in two ways:

a) using properties: <property name="endDate" *column="END_DATE" type="timestamp" index="IDX_END_DATE"/*>

b) using annotations, as a Hibernate extension:

```
@Column(name = "END_DATE", nullable = false, updatable = false)
@org.hibernate.annotations.Index(name = "IDX_END_DATE")
private Date endDate;
```

50: What are the transient objects?

Answer:

Objects instantiated using the new operator aren't immediately persistent. Their state is transient/ which means they aren't associated with any database table row and so their state is lost as soon as they're no longer referenced by any other object. These objects have a lifespan that effectively ends at that time, and they become inaccessible and available for garbage collection.

51: What is a persistent object?

Answer:

A persistent instance is an entity instance with a database identity. Persistent instances may be objects instantiated by the application and then made persistent by calling one of the methods on the persistence manager.

52: What is the persistence context? Why is it useful?

Answer:

The persistence context is a cache of managed entity instances. It is useful for several reasons:

a) Hibernate can do automatic dirty checking and transactional write-behind.

b) Hibernate can use the persistence context as a first-level cache.

c) Hibernate can guarantee a scope of Java object identity.

d) Hibernate can extend the persistence context to span a whole conversation.

53: Define the Hibernate conversations concept.

Answer:

A conversation is an implementation of a possibly long-running unit of work. Conversations are used in order to keep database transactions short and release database resources as soon as possible, while the user completes a unit of work (for example, filling an online form). There are two strategies available to implement a conversation in a Hibernate application: with detached objects or by extending a persistence context.

54: What is a business key?

Answer:

A business key is a property, or some combination of properties, that is unique for each instance with the same database identity. Unlike a natural primary key/ it isn't an absolute requirement that the business key never changes — as long as it changes rarely, that's enough. As an example/ for the User class, username is a great candidate business key.

55: Which services provide Hibernate's persistence manager API?

Answer:

Hibernate persistence manager provides the following services:

a) basic CRUD (create, retrieve, update, delete) operations
b) query execution
c) control of transactions
d) management of the persistence context

It is exposed by several different interfaces: Session, Query, Criteria and Transaction.

56: Describe Hibernate replication mechanism. Provide a short replication example.

Answer:

Replication is the mechanism that allows retrieving objects from one database and storing them into another. It takes detached objects loaded in one Session and makes them persistent in another Session. These Sessions are usually opened from two different SessionFactorys that have been configured with a mapping for the same persistent class. Here is an example:

```
Session session = sessionFactory1.openSession();
Transaction tx = session.beginTransaction();
Item item = (Item) session.get(Item.class, new Long(1234));
tx.commit();
session.close();
Session session2 = sessionFactory2.openSession();
Transaction tx2 = session2.beginTransaction();
```

```
session2.replicate(item, ReplicationMode.LATEST_VERSION);
tx2.commit();
session2.close();
```

57: What is the purpose/usage of Hibernate ReplicationMode?

Answer:

The ReplicationMode controls the details of the replication procedure:

a) *ReplicationMode.IGNORE* – ignores the object when there is an existing database row with the same identifier in the target database.

b) *ReplicationMode.OVERWRITE* – overwrites any existing database row with the same identifier in the target database.

c) *ReplicationMode.EXCEPTION* – throws an exception if there is an existing database row with the same identifier in the target database.

d) *ReplicationMode.LATEST_VERSION* – overwrites the row in the target database if its version is earlier than the version of the object, or ignores the object otherwise. Requires enabled Hibernate optimistic concurrency control.

58: In which cases do Hibernate flushes occur?

Answer:

They occur at the following times:

a) when a Transaction on the Hibernate API is committed

b) before a query is executed

c) when the application calls session.flush() explicitly

59: Which are the typed exceptions are thrown by Hibernate?

Answer:

Hibernate throws the following subtypes of RuntimeException:

a) *HibernateException* - a generic error. In order to find out more about the cause the developer must call getCause() on the exception.

b) *JDBCException* - any exception thrown by Hibernate's internal JDBC layer. This kind of exception is always caused by a particular SQL statement, and can the offending statement can be got with getSQL().

c) subtypes of JDBCException and an internal converter that tries to translate the vendor-specific error code thrown by the database driver into something more meaningful. The built-in converter can produce JDBCConnectionException, SQLGrammarException, LockAquisitionException, DataException, and ConstraintViolationException .

d) *other RuntimeExceptions* - should also abort a transaction.

60: Which configuration options must be set in order to enable CMT with Hibernate?

Answer:

a) the hibernate.transaction.factory_class option must be set to org.hibernate.transaction.CMTTransactionFactory.

b) hibernate.transaction.manager_lookup_class must be set to the right lookup class for each application server.

61: Which Hibernate configuration option sets the JDBC connections isolation levels?

Answer:

hibernate.connection.isolation option. It may have the following values:

a) 1 – read uncommitted isolation
b) 2 – read committed isolation
c) 4 – repeatable read isolation
d) 8 – serializable isolation

62: Which are the LockModes supported by Hibernate?

Answer:

Hibernate supports the following additional LockModes:

a) *LockMode.NONE* – don't go to the database unless the object isn't in any cache.

b) *LockMode.READ* – bypass all caches, and perform a version check to verify that the object in memory is the same version that currently exists in the database.

c) *LockMode.UPDGRADE* – bypass all caches, do a version check (if applicable), and obtain a database-level pessimistic upgrade lock, if that is supported.

d) *LockMode.UPDGRADE_NOWAIT* – disables waiting for concurrent lock releases, thus throwing a locking exception immediately if the lock can't be obtained.

e) *LockMode.FORCE* – forces an increment of the objects version in the database, to indicate that it has been modified by the current transaction.

f) *LockMode.WRITE* – obtained automatically when Hibernate has written to a row in the current transaction.

63: How to implement a conversation that doesn't involve detached objects?

Answer:

This can be done by extending the persistence context to span the whole conversation. The operation is known as the session-per-conversation strategy.

64: What is the transitive persistence?

Answer:

Transitive persistence is a technique that allows you to propagate persistence to transient and detached subgraphs automatically. It is useful in real, nontrivial applications that work not only with single objects, but rather with networks of objects. When the application manipulates a network of persistent objects, the result may be an object graph consisting of persistent, detached, and transient instances.

65: Which is the difference between Hibernate Query Language (HQL)and SQL?

Answer:

The main difference between the two is that HQL uses class names instead of table names, and property names instead of column names. It also understands inheritance, whether the query is performed with a superclass or an interface.

66: In which context is StatelessSession used?

Answer:

StatelessSession is an alternative interface used in order to provide working with the database by executing statements. This statement-oriented interface feels and works like plain JDBC, except that you get the benefit from mapped persistent classes and Hibernate's database portability.

67: Which ways to get objects out of the database does Hibernate provide?

Answer:

This can be done using one of the following methods:

a) navigating the object graph, starting from an already loaded object, by accessing the associated objects through property accessor methods.

b) retrieval by identifier, the most convenient method when the unique identifier value of an object is known.

c) the Hibernate Query Language (HQL), which is a full object-oriented query language.

d) the Hibernate Criteria interface, which provides a type-safe and object-oriented way to perform queries without the need for string manipulation.

e) native SQL queries, including stored procedure calls, where Hibernate still takes care of mapping the JDBC result sets to graphs of persistent objects.

68: Shortly describe Hibernate's cache architecture.

Answer:

Hibernate has a two-level cache architecture:

a) the first-level cache is the persistence context cache. This is a mandatory first-level cache that also guarantees the scope of object and database identity.

b) the second-level cache in Hibernate is pluggable and may be scoped to the process or cluster. This is a cache of state (returned by value), not of actual persistent instances.

c) Hibernate also implements a cache for query result sets that integrates closely with the second-level cache; this is an optional feature.

69: Which open source cache providers are built into Hibernate?

Answer:

a) *EHCache* - a cache provider intended for a simple process scope cache in a single JVM. It can cache in memory or on disk, and it supports the optional Hibernate query result cache.

b) *OpenSymphony OSCache* - a service that supports caching to memory and disk in a single JVM, with a rich set of expiration policies and query cache support.

c) *SwarmCache* - a cluster cache based on JGroups. It uses clustered invalidation but doesn't support the Hibernate query cache.

d) *JBoss Cache* - a fully transactional replicated clustered cache also based on the JGroups multicast library. It supports replication or invalidation, synchronous or asynchronous communication, and optimistic and pessimistic locking. The Hibernate query cache is supported, assuming that clocks are synchronized in the cluster.

70: How can Hibernate be accessed using Spring ?

Answer:

Extending HibernateDaoSupport and applying an AOP Interceptor or using HibernateTemplate and Callback (IoC).

Spring

71: What is Dependency Injection/Inversion of Control? How is this core concept implemented in Spring framework?

Answer:

Dependency Injection is a design pattern that decouples highly dependent components. In Spring Framework, it is implemented using BeanFactory interface which decouples the configuration and specification of dependencies from the actual program logic.

72: Which tools offers Spring framework in order to achieve IoC?

Answer:

a) *Interface Dependency* - beans must implement specific interfaces to have their dependencies managed by the container.

b) *Setter Injection* - dependencies and properties are configured through a bean's setter methods.

c) *Constructor Injection* - dependencies and properties are configured through the bean's constructor.

73: What is AOP? What is the difference between AOP and OOP?

Answer:

Aspect Oriented Programming. In OOP the application is decomposed into a hierarchy of objects, in AOP the application is decomposed into aspects or concerns.

74: Which are the core AOP Concepts?

Answer:

The core AOP concepts are:

a) *Aspect:* A modularization of a concern for which the implementation might otherwise cut across multiple objects (for e.g. transaction management)

b) *Joinpoint:* Point during the execution of a program, such as a method invocation or a particular exception being thrown.

c) *Advice:* Action taken by the AOP framework at a particular joinpoint.

d) *Pointcut:* A set of joinpoints specifying when an advice should fire.

e) *Introduction:* Adding methods or fields to an advised class.

f) *Proxied object:* Object containing the joinpoint.

g) *AOP proxy:* Object created by the AOP framework, including advice.

h) *Weaving:* Assembling aspects to create an advised object.

75: What are the main Advice types?

Answer:

a) *"around":* the most general and powerful kind of service, is an advice that surrounds a joinpoint such as a method invocation.

b) *"before":* advice that executes before a joinpoint, but

which does not have the ability to prevent execution flow proceeding to the joinpoint (unless it throws an exception).

c) *"after":* advice to be executed regardless of the means by which a join point exits (normal or exceptional return).

d) *"throws":* advice to be executed if a method throws an exception.

e) *"introduction":* adds new methods (and attributes) to the target object

76: Enumerate several methods from BeanFactory interface.

Answer:

a) Boolean containsBean(String name)
b) String[] getAliases(String name)
c) Object getBean(String name)
d) Object getBean(String name, Class requiredType)
e) Class getType(String name)
f) boolean isPrototype(String name)
g) boolean isSingleton(String name)
h) boolean isTypeMatch(String name, Class targetType)

77: Which is the most commonly used simple BeanFactory implementation? Give an example for creating such an object.

Answer:

XmlBeanFactory, which loads its beans based on the definitions contained in an XML file. Example: *BeanFactory factory = new XmlBeanFactory(new FileInputStream("beans.xml"));*

78: How can a bean be retrieved from a BeanFactory?

Answer:

Calling the getBean() method, passing the name of the bean which will be retrieved.

Example: *MyBean myBean = (MyBean) factory.getBean("myBean");*

79: What is the relation between BeanFactory and ApplicationContext?

Answer:

ApplicationContext extends BeanFactory. BeanFactory provides basic functionality and the configuration framework, while ApplicationContext adds enhanced capabilities like message resource handling, event propagation, an easier integration with AOP features, and creation of application-layer specific contexts.

80: How can a bean be identified within ApplicationContext?

Answer:

A bean is identified by its id and name. It can have multiple ids (the extra ids are considered aliases) but these ids must be unique within the BeanFactory or ApplicationContext the bean is hosted in.

81: Which are the most commonly used implementations of ApplicationContext? When should they be used?

Answer:

a) *ClassPathXmlApplicationContext* – Will be used when

loading a context definition from an XML file located in the class path; it treats context definition files as class path resources.

b) *FileSystemXmlApplicationContext* – Used when loading a context definition from an XML file in the filesystem.

c) *XmlWebApplicationContext* – Used when loading context definitions from an XML file contained within a web application.

82: Which is the difference between uses of FileSystemXmlApplicationContext and ClassPathXmlApplicationContext?

Answer:

FileSystemXmlApplicationContext will look for context definition in a specific location, whereas ClassPathXmlApplicationContext will look for the context definition anywhere in the class path.

83: Which is the difference between an application context and a bean factory regarding how singleton beans are loaded?

Answer:

When a bean factory is used, all the beans are lazily loaded and the bean creation is deferred until the getBean() method is called. The application context preloads all singleton beans upon context startup - this way, you ensure that the beans will be ready to use when needed and the application won't have to wait for them to be created.

84: Which is the difference regarding lifecycle between a traditional Java bean and a bean within a Spring container?

Answer:

The life cycle of a traditional Java bean is fairly simple. Java's new keyword is used to instantiate the bean and it's ready to use. In contrast, the life cycle of a bean within a Spring container is a bit more elaborate.

85: Which is the lifecycle of a bean in Spring context?

Answer:

a) The container finds the bean's definition and instantiates the bean.

b) Using dependency injection, Spring populates all of the properties as specified in the bean definition.

c) If the bean implements the BeanNameAware interface, the factory calls setBeanName() passing the bean's ID.

d) If the bean implements the BeanFactoryAware interface, the factory calls setBeanFactory(), passing an instance of itself.

e) If there are any BeanPostProcessors associated with the bean, their postProcessBeforeInitialization() methods will be called.

f) If an init-method is specified for the bean, it will be called.

g) Finally, if there are any BeanPostProcessors associated

with the bean, their postProcessAfterInitialization() methods will be called.

86: What does "wiring" mean?

Answer:

Wiring is the operation of piecing together the beans within the Spring container. When wiring beans, the container is told what beans are needed and how it should use dependency injection in order to tie them together.

87: Which Spring containers support wiring through XML?

Answer:

a) *XmlBeanFactory* – a simple BeanFactory that loads a context definition file by way of a java.io.InputStream.

b) *ClassPathXmlApplicationContext* – an application context that loads the context definition file from the class path.

c) *FileSystemXmlApplicationContext* – an application context that loads the context definition file from the file system.

d) *XmlWebApplicationContext* – an application context used with Springenabled web applications that loads the context definition file from a web application context.

88: Can you recognize the purpose of the following xml file?

```
<?xml version="1.0" encoding="UTF-8"?>
<beans>
 <bean id="b1" class="com.springinaction.Bean1"/>
```

```
<bean id="b2" class="com.springinaction.Bean2"/>
</beans>
```

Answer:

It is a trivial context definition file which configures two beans, b1 and b2, in the Spring container.

89: Which are the methods provided by InitializingBean and DisposableBean interfaces?

Answer:

InitializingBean provides method afterPropertiesSet(), that will be called once all of a bean's properties have been set. Similarly/ DisposableBean's one method/ destroy()/ will be called when the bean is removed from the container.

90: What is a setter injection?

Answer:

It is a technique for populating a bean's properties based on standard naming conventions (JavaBean specification formalized the well-practiced idiom of having "set" and "get" methods that are used to set and retrieve a bean property's value).

91: Could you provide an example of setter injection?

Answer:

```
<bean id="b1" class="com.test.Bean1"
 <property name="name"><value>Test Bean</value>
 </property>
</bean>
```

This sample code sets the name property by calling setName("Test Bean")

92: Does Spring framework offer any alternative to setter injection?

Answer:

Yes, the alternative is constructor injection.

93: What is the similarity and difference between setter and constructor injection?

Answer:

With setter injection, the properties injected are defined with the <property> subelement. Constructor injection is similar, excepting the case when <constructor-arg> subelement of <bean> will be used in order to specify arguments to pass to a bean's constructor at instantiation. One difference between these two is that the<constructor-arg> does not contain a name attribute, thing that the <property> subelement did.

94: What does the following code do?

```
<bean id="b2" class="com.test.Bean2"
 <constructor-arg><value>100</value>
 </constructor-arg>
</bean>
```

Answer:

This is an example of constructor injection configuration. It constructs a Bean2 object.

95: Supposing you have a class Test defined as following:

public class Test { public Test(String arg1, java.net.URL arg2) {} }

And a bean wired in the following way:

```
<bean id="test" class="com.springinaction.Test">
 <constructor-arg>
  <value>http://url1.com</value>
 </constructor-arg>
 <constructor-arg>
  <value>http://url2.com</value>
 </constructor-arg>
</bean
```

Which will be the compilation result? Motivate your answer.

Answer:

Spring will throw an org.springframework.beans.factory. UnsatisfiedDependencyException, indicating that there is an ambiguity in the constructor arguments.

It can be solved by adding index or type attributes to constructor arguments.

96: Why constructor injection is used? What will be counter arguments in using it?

Answer:

Arguments:

a) *because it enforces a strong dependency contract* - a bean cannot be instantiated without being provided all of its dependencies.

b) the code lines are at a minimum due to the fact that all of the bean's dependencies are set through its constructor and there is no need for setter methods.

c) due to the fact that the properties are set through the constructor, these properties become immutable.

Counter arguments:

a) if a bean has several dependencies/ the constructor's parameter list can become very long.

b) if there are multiple constructors for an object, it could be hard to come up with unique constructors since constructor signatures vary only by the number and type of parameters.

c) if a constructor takes two or more parameters of the same type, it may be difficult to determine what is the purpose of each parameter

97: What is the benefit of autowiring?

Answer:

The programmer doesn't have to wire all of the bean's properties explicitly using the <property> element; instead, Spring wire the beans automatically by setting the autowire property on each <bean> wanted as autowired.

98: What are the four types of autowiring?

Answer:

a) *byName* – the container tries to find a bean whose name (or ID) is the same as the name of the property being wired. If a matching bean is not found, then the property will remain unwired.

b) *byType* – attempts to find a single bean in the container whose type matches the type of the property being wired. If no matching bean is found, then the property will not be wired. If more than one bean matches, an org.springrframework.beans.factory.UnsatisfiedDependencyException will be thrown.

c) *constructor* – Tries to match up one or more beans in the container with the parameters of one of the constructors of the bean being wired. In the event of ambiguous beans or ambiguous constructors, an org.springframework.beans.factory.UnsatisfiedDependencyException will be thrown.

d) *autodetect* – Attempts to autowire by constructor first and then using byType. Ambiguity is handled the same way as with constructor and byType wiring.

99: How are pointcuts defined in Spring?

Answer:

Pointcuts are defined in terms of class and method that is being advised. Advice is woven into the target class and its methods are based on their characteristics, such as class name and method signature. The core interface for Spring's pointcut framework is the Pointcut interface.

100: Why static pointcuts are preferred over dynamic ones?

Answer:

Static pointcuts are preferred because they perform better since they are evaluated once (when the proxy is created); dynamic pointcuts are evaluated at each runtime invocation.

101: Which class/method needs to be implemented in order to create a custom static pointcut?

Answer:

Abstract class StaticMethodMatcherPointcut needs to be extended and isMatch() method should be overriden.

102: Which is the built-in dynamic pointcut offered by Spring?

Answer:

ControlFlowPointcut. This pointcut matches based on information about the current thread's call stack/ thus it can be configured to return true only if a particular method or class is found in the current thread's stack of execution.

103: Which class/method needs to be implemented in order to create a custom dynamic pointcut?

Answer:

Interface MethodMatcher should be implemented and isRuntime() method should return true. This effectively makes the pointcut dynamic and the matches(Method m, Class target, Object[] args) method will be called for every method invocation this pointcut evaluates.

104: Enumerate several pointcut types supported by Spring framework?

Answer:

AbstractExpressionPointcut, AbstractRegexpMethodPointcut, AnnotationMatchingPointcut, AspectJExpressionPointcut, ComposablePointcut, ControlFlowPointcut, DynamicMethodMatcherPointcut, dkRegexpMethodPointcut, NameMatchMethodPointcut, Perl5RegexpMethodPointcut, StaticMethodMatcherPointcut. All these classes implement Pointcut interface.

105: How are Introductions implemented in Spring?

Answer:

They are implemented through a special interface: IntroductionMethodInterceptor.

106: When would somebody use ProxyFactoryBean objects? Describe several ProxyFactoryBean properties.

Answer:

When a proxy object is needed. Below are listed some of the most common used class properties:

a) *target* - the target bean of the proxy.

b) *proxyInterfaces* - a list of interfaces that should be implemented by the proxy.

c) *interceptorNames* - the bean names of the advice to be applied to the target. These can be names of interceptors, advisors, or any other advice type.

d) *singleton* - whether the factory should return the same instance of the proxy for each get-Bean invocation. If stateful advice is used, this should be set to false.

e) *exposeProxy* - whether the target class should have access to the current proxy. This is done by calling AopContext.getCurrentProxy.

107: Which are the two Spring classes that provide autoproxy support?

Answer:

BeanNameAutoProxyCreator, which generates proxies for beans that match a set of names and DefaultAdvisorAutoProxyCreator, the more powerful autoproxy creator.

108: Which is the most common use for metadata autoproxying?

Answer:

Metadata autoproxying is mostly used for declarative transaction support via AOP framework. This powerful framework offers the same capabilities as EJB's declarative transactions.

109: What are the advantages of accessing the DAOs through interfaces?

Answer:

a) the service objects are easily testable since they are not coupled to a specific data access implementation

b) data access tier is accessed in a persistence technology-agnostic manner

110: What kind of exceptions does Spring's DAO frameworks throw?

Answer:

Spring's DAO frameworks doesn't throw technology-specific exceptions, such as SQLException or HibernateException. Instead, all exceptions thrown are subclasses of the technology-agnostic org.springframework.dao.DataAccessException.

111: Which Spring interface is responsible for mapping a ResultSet row to an object? Give a short example.

Answer:

RowMapper interface.

```
class PersonRowMapper implements RowMapper {
 public Object mapRow(ResultSet rs, int index) throws SQLException {
  Person person = new Person();
  person.setId(new Integer(rs.getInt("id")));
  person.setFirstName(rs.getString("first_name"));
  person.setLastName(rs.getString("last_name"));
  return person;
 }
}
```

112: Which is the difference between Spring's support for programmatic transaction management and the one offered by EJB?

Answer:

a) Unlike EJB, which is coupled with a Java Transaction API (JTA) implementation, Spring employs a callback mechanism that abstracts the actual transaction implementation from the transactional code.

b) Although both EJB and Spring allow definition of transaction boundaries declaratively, Spring goes beyond the container-managed transactions by allowing declaration of additional attributes such as isolation level and timeouts.

113: Give example of several Spring transaction managers and their usage.

Answer:

a) DataSourceTransactionManager - Manages transactions on a single JDBC DataSource.

b) HibernateTransactionManager - Used to manage transactions when Hibernate is the persistence mechanism.

c) JdoTransactionManager - Used to manage transactions when JDO is used for persistence.

d) JtaTransactionManager - Manages transactions using a Java Transaction API (JTA) implementatio n. Must be used when a transaction spans multiple resources.

e) PersistenceBrokerTransactionManager - Manages transactions when Apache's Object Relational Bridge (OJB) is used for persistence.

114: What is a Spring transaction attribute?

Answer:

It is a description of how transaction policies should be applied to a method. This description could include one or more of the following parameters:

a) Propagation behavior
b) Isolation level
c) Read-only hints
d) The transaction timeout period

115: Which are the RPC models supported by Spring?

Answer:

Spring supports remoting for six different RPC models: Remote Method Invocation(RMI)/ Caucho's Hessian and Burlap/ Spring's own HTTP invoker/ EJB/ and web services using JAX-RPC.

116: How does Spring provide support for EJB?

Answer:

Spring provides support for EJBs in two ways:

a) by enabling declaration of EJBs as beans within the Spring configuration file. This makes it possible to wire EJB references into the properties of other beans as though the EJB was just another POJO.
b) by allowing to write EJBs that act as a façade to Spring-configured beans.

117: Which mechanisms provide Spring in order to access EJBs?

Answer:

Spring provides two proxy factory beans that provide access to EJBs:

a) *LocalStatelessSessionProxyFactoryBean* – Used to access local EJBs (EJBs in the same container as their clients).

b) *SimpleRemoteStatelessSessionProxyFactoryBean* – Used to access remote EJBs (EJBs that are in a separate container from their clients).

118: Which support classes offers Spring in order to ease the development of EJBs?

Answer:

Spring provides four abstract support classes to make developing EJBs a little bit easier:

a) *AbstractMessageDrivenBean* – useful for developing message-driven beans that accept messages from sources other than JMS (as allowed by the EJB 2.1 specification)

b) *AbstractJmsMessageDrivenBean* – useful for developing message-driven beans that accept messages from JMS sources

c) *AbstractStatefulSessionBean* – useful for developing stateful session EJBs

d) *AbstractStatelessSessionBean* – useful for developing stateless session EJBs

119: How does Spring offer JNDI support along with all of the benefits of dependency injection?

Answer:

Through class JndiObjectFactoryBean which extends JndiObjectLocator and implements FactoryBean. It is a factory bean, which means that when it is wired into a property, it will actually create some other type of object that will wire into that property. In the case of JndiObjectFactoryBean, it will wire an object retrieved from JNDI.

120: How does Spring offer e-mail support?

Answer:

Through MailSender *interface and its two implementations:*

a) *CosMailSenderImpl* – simple implementation of an SMTP mail sender

b) *JavaMailSenderImpl* – a JavaMail API-based implementation of a mail sender which allows sending MIME messages as well as non-SMTP mail (such as Lotus Notes).

121: What is a MVC front controller? Which is Spring's MVC front controller servlet?

Answer:

A front controller is a common web-application pattern where a single servlet delegates responsibility for a request to other components of an application to perform the actual processing. In the case of Spring MVC, DispatcherServlet is the front controller.

122: Which is the interface implemented by all Spring MVC's handlers?

Answer:

HandlerMapping interface. Spring comes prepackaged with three useful implementations of HandlerMapping:

a) *BeanNameUrlHandlerMapping* – maps controllers to URLs that are based on the controllers' bean name

b) *SimpleUrlHandlerMapping* – maps controllers to URLs using a property collection defined in the context configuration file

c) *CommonsPathMapHandlerMapping* – maps controllers to URLs using sourcelevel metadata placed in the controller code

123: Describe several Spring controller classes and their usage.

Answer:

a) *Controller, AbstractController* - the controller is extremely simple, requiring little more functionality than is afforded by basic Java servlets.

b) *ThrowawayController* - offers a simple way to handle requests as commands (in a manner similar to WebWork Actions).

c) *MultiActionController* - used if the application has several actions that perform similar or related logic.

d) *BaseCommandController, AbstractCommandController* - used weather the controller accepts one or more parameters from the request and bind them to an object. It is also capable of performing parameter validation.

e) *AbstractFormController, SimpleFormController* - used if

there is needed to display an entry form to the user and also process the data entered into the form.

f) *AbstractWizardFormController* - used in order to walk through a complex, multipage entry form that ultimately gets processed as a single form.

124: Define a Spring form controller. What is it used for?

Answer:

A form controller takes the concept of command controller a step further by adding functionality to display a form when an HTTP GET request is received and process the form when an HTTP POST is received. Furthermore, if any errors occur in processing the form, the controller will know to redisplay the form so that the user can correct the errors and resubmit.

125: What is the interface that accommodates validation for Spring MVC? Describe its main methods.

Answer:

Validator interface. It has two methods:

a) *void validate(Object obj, Errors errors)* - examines the fields of the object passed and rejects any invalid values via the Errors object

b) *boolean supports(Class clazz)* - used to help Spring determine whether or not the validator can be used for a given class.

126: Which class must be extended in order to construct a

wizard controller? Which are the compulsory methods of this class?

Answer:

AbstractWizardFormController class. The only compulsory method of AbstractWizardFormController is processFinish() which is called to finalize the form when the user has finished completing it.

127: Which is the difference between the wizard controllers and the other command controllers?

Answer:

With other command controllers, the command object is completely populated at once. But with wizard controllers, the command object is populated as the user steps through the wizard's pages. Another difference is that unlike the other command controllers, wizard controllers never call the standard validate() method of their Validator object.

128: Give an example of a Spring controller which is able to perform multiple actions.

Answer:

Such a controller would be MultiActionController - a special type of controller that is able to perform multiple actions, with each action being dispatched to a different method.

129: Which is Spring's default method name resolver? Give example of other method name resolvers.

Answer:

Spring's default method name resolver is InternalPathMethodNameResolver, which resolves method names based on URL patterns. Other method name resolvers are:

a) *ParameterMethodNameResolver* – resolves the execution method name based on a parameter in the request

b) *PropertiesMethodNameResolver* – resolves the name of the execution method by consulting a list of key/value pairs

130: How can a view be defined in Spring MVC?

Answer:

In Spring MVC, a view is a bean that renders results to the user.

131: Which are Spring implementations of ViewResolver?

Answer:

a) *InternalResourceViewResolver* – resolves logical view names into View objects that are rendered using template file resources (such as JSPs and Velocity templates)

b) *BeanNameViewResolver* – resolves logical view names into View beans in the DispatcherServlet's application context

c) *ResourceBundleViewResolver* – resolves logical view names into View objects contained in a ResourceBundle

d) *XmlViewResolver* – resolves View beans from an XML file that is separate from the DispatcherServlet's application context

132: What is BeanNameViewResolver?

Answer:

BeanNameViewResolver is a view resolver that matches logical view names up with names of beans in the application context.

133: Which class supports the creation of PDF files as views in Spring MVC?

Answer:

Class AbstractPdfView is an abstract implementation of a View that supports the creation of PDF files as views in Spring MVC. In order to be used, it must inherit class AbstractPdfView and implement the buildPdfDocument() method.

134: What is the Spring API used for manipulating PDF documents?

Answer:

iText, a library that allows you to create and manipulate PDF documents. It enables developers looking to enhance web and other applications with dynamic PDF document generation and/or manipulation. It can be used for multiple purposes like serving PDF to a browser, generating dynamic documents from XML files or databases, addition of bookmarks, page numbers, watermarks, digital signatures etc.

135: What is Acegi Security System?

Answer:

Acegi is a security framework that provides declarative security for Spring based applications. It provides a collection of beans that are configured within a Spring application context/ taking full advantage of Spring's support for dependency injection and aspect-oriented programming.

136: Which is the main mechanism used by Acegi in order to secure web applications?

Answer:

When securing web applications, Acegi uses servlet filters that intercept servlet requests to perform authentication and enforce security. It also employs a unique mechanism that enables injection with their dependencies using Spring IoC.

137: Which are the mechanisms offered by Acegi in order to authenticate against a database?

Answer:

Acegi has two very useful authentication providers:

a) DaoAuthenticationProvider
b) PasswordDaoAuthenticationProvider

Both of these authentication providers enable verifying a user's identity by comparing their principal and credentials against the database entries.

138: Which is the difference between *DaoAuthenticationProvider* &

PasswordDaoAuthenticationProvider?

Answer:

The difference among the two authentication providers is in where the actual authentication takes place. A DaoAuthenticationProvider uses its DAO to retrieve the username and password, which it then uses to authenticate the user. PasswordDaoAuthenticationProvider pushes responsibility for authentication off to its DAO.

139: What are the password encoders provided by Acegi?

Answer:

Acegi provides three password encoders:

a) *PlaintextPasswordEncoder (default)* – performs no encoding on the password, returning it unaltered.

b) *Md5PasswordEncoder* – performs Message Digest (MD5) encoding on the password.

c) *ShaPasswordEncoder* – performs Secure Hash Algorithm encoding on the password.

140: Which are the Acegi implementations of CasProxyDecider?

Answer:

a) *AcceptAnyCasProxy* – accepts a proxy request from any service

b) *NamedCasProxyDecider* – accepts proxy requests from those in a list of named services

c) *RejectProxyTickets* – rejects all proxy requests

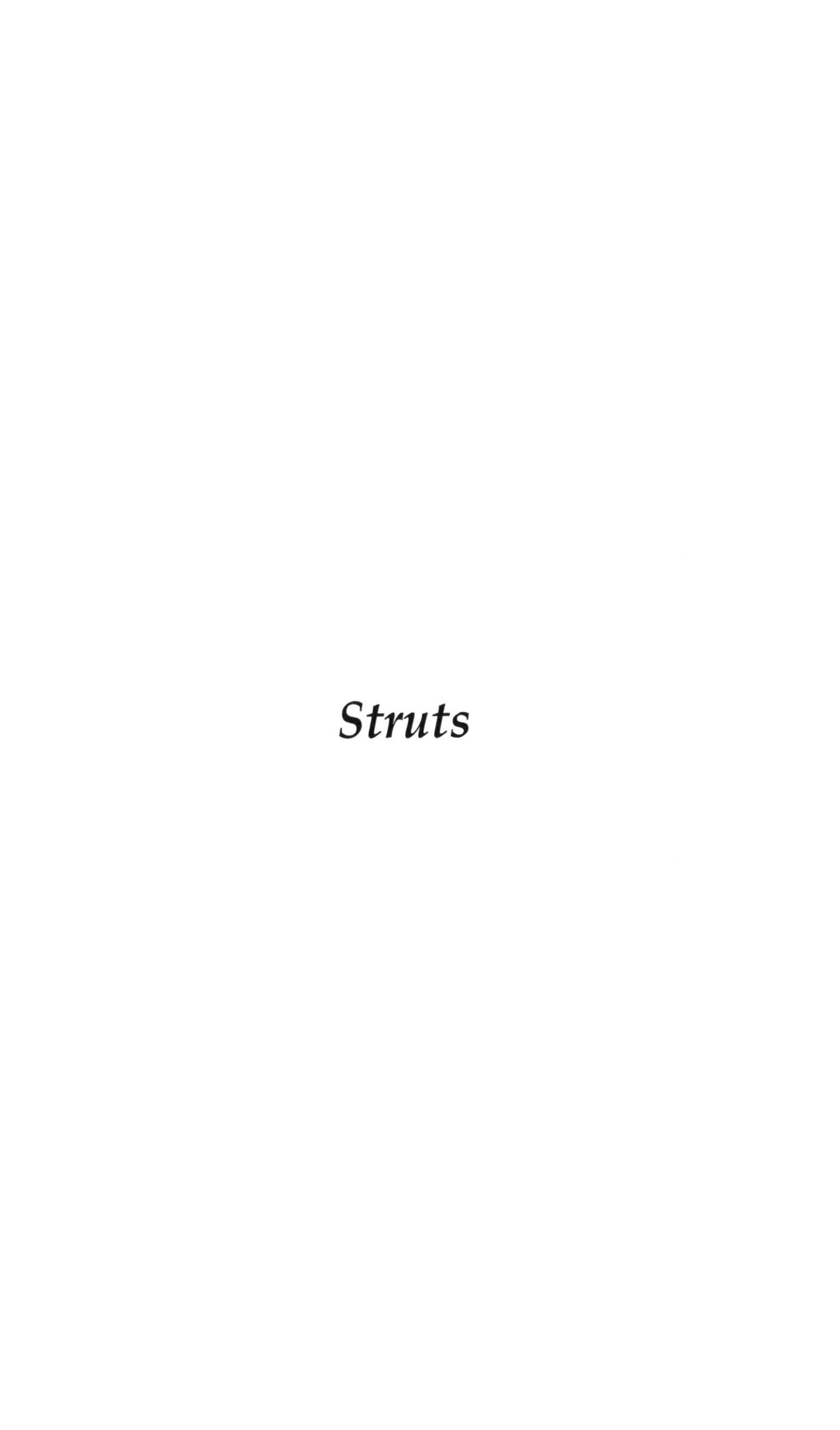

Struts

141: What design pattern does Struts implement?

Answer:

Struts is a second-generation web application framework that implements the Model-View-Controller (MVC) design pattern.

142: What architectural features are introduced by Struts?

Answer:

Struts introduces several architectural features that make the framework cleaner and more flexible. These new features include:

a) interceptors for layering cross-cutting concerns away from action logic

b) annotation-based configuration to reduce or eliminate XML configuration

c) a powerful expression language, Object-Graph Navigation Language (OGNL), that transverses the entire framework

d) a mini-MVC–based tag API that supports modifiable and reusable UI components.

143: What does Struts 2 framework bring in comparison with Struts 1?

Answer:

Struts 2 comes with improvements in the following areas:

a) *Action classes:* Struts 1 requires Action classes to extend an abstract base class while a Struts 2 Action may implement an Action interface.

b) *Threading Model:* Struts 1 Actions are singletons and must be thread-safe; Struts 2 Action objects are instantiated for each request, so there are no thread-safety issues.

c) *Servlet Dependency:* Struts 1 Actions have dependencies on the servlet API while Struts 2 Actions are not coupled to a container.

d) *Testability:* Testing Struts 1 Actions exposes the Servlet API while Struts 2 Actions can be tested by instantiating the Action, setting properties, and invoking methods

e) *Harvesting Input:* Struts 1 uses an ActionForm object to capture input while Struts 2 uses Action properties as input properties, eliminating the need for a second input object.

f) *Expression Language:* Struts 1 integrates with JSTL, so it uses the JSTL EL. Struts 2 can use JSTL, but the framework also supports a more powerful and flexible expression language called "Object Graph Notation Language" (OGNL).

g) *Binding values into views:* Struts 1 uses the standard JSP mechanism for binding objects into the page context for access while Struts 2 uses a "ValueStack" technology so that the taglibs can access values without coupling your view to the object type it is rendering.

h) *Type Conversion:* Struts 1 ActionForm properties are usually all Strings while Struts 2 uses OGNL for type conversion.

i) *Validation:* Struts 1 supports manual validation via a validate method on the ActionForm or through an extension to the Commons Validator while Struts 2 supports manual validation via the validate method and the XWork Validation framework.

j) *Control Of Action Execution:* Struts 1 supports separate Request Processors (lifecycles) for each module, but all the Actions in the module must share the same lifecycle while Struts 2 supports creating different lifecycles on a per Action basis via Interceptor Stacks.

144: How are MVC concerns implemented in Struts framework?

Answer:

In Struts 2 model, view, and controller are implemented as action, result, and FilterDispatcher.

145: Which is the role of a Struts action?

Answer:

A Struts action serves two roles. First, an action is an encapsulation of the calls to business logic into a single unit of work. Second, the action serves as a locus of data transfer.

146: What are the Struts interceptors?

Answer:

Interceptors are components that execute both before and after the rest of the request processing. They provide an architectural component in which to define various workflow and cross-cutting tasks so that they can be easily reused as well as separated from other architectural concerns.

147: What is the Object-Graph Navigation Language?

Answer:

OGNL is a tool that allows accessing the data put in a central repository. More specifically, it is an expression language that allows referencing and manipulating the data on the ValueStack.

148: What is the ValueStack?

Answer:

ValueStack is a storage area for all application domain data that will be needed during the processing of a request. Data is moved to the ValueStack in preparation for request processing, it is manipulated there during action execution, and it is read from there when the results render their response pages.

149: Which are the mechanisms for declaring the architecture of a Struts application?

Answer:

The architecture of a Struts application can be declared in two ways: through XML-based configuration files or through Java annotations.

150: Which is the purpose of the intelligent defaults?

Answer:

Intelligent defaults provide out-of-the-box components that solve common domain workflows without requiring further configuration by the developer, allowing the most common application tasks to be realized with minimum development.

151: Which are the most important elements in the deployment descriptor for a Struts application?

Answer:

For a Struts 2 application, the most important elements in the deployment descriptor are the filter and filter-mapping elements that set up the Struts 2 FilterDispatcher. This servlet filter is basically the Struts 2 framework. FilterDispatcher examines all the incoming requests looking for requests that target Struts 2 actions.

152: What does a Struts action do?

Answer:

Struts actions do three things:

a) encapsulate the actual work to be done for a given request using execute() method

b) serve as a data carrier in the framework's automatic transfer of data from the request to the view

c) assist the framework in determining which result should render the view that'll be returned in the request response.

153: Which are the constants defined by the Action interface?

Answer:

a) public static final String ERROR "error"

b) public static final String INPUT "input"

c) public static final String LOGIN "login"
d) public static final String NONE "none"
e) public static final String SUCCESS "success"

154: Give an example of a class that provides default implementations of the Action interface.

Answer:

ActionSupport, a class that provides a quick form of basic validation that will serve well in many cases. It implements also some useful interfaces like LocaleProvider, TextProvider, Validateable, ValidationAware, Serializable.

155: How does Struts offer support for localizing message text?

Answer:

Through LocaleProvider interface which exposes a single method, getLocale(). ActionSupport implements this interface to retrieve the user's locale based upon the locale setting sent in by the browser.

156: What are the ModelDriven actions?

Answer:

ModelDriven actions depart from the use of JavaBeans properties for exposing domain data. They expose an application domain object via the getModel() method, which is declared by the ModelDriven interface.

157: What is the potential danger in using domain objects for data transfer?

Answer:

A problem might come when the data gets automatically transferred onto the object. If the request has parameters that match the attributes on the domain object, the data will be moved onto those attributes. Considering the case where the domain object has some sensitive data attributes that shouldn't be exposed to this automatic data transfer, a malicious user could add an appropriately named querystring parameter to the request such that the value of that parameter would automatically be written to the exposed object's attribute.

158: What does the fileUpload interceptor do?

Answer:

The fileUpload interceptor creates a special version of the automatic data transfer mechanisms. When the fileUpload interceptor executes, it processes a multipart request and transforms the file itself, along with some metadata, into request parameters. It does this using a wrapper around the servlet request.

159: Which is the interface which orchestrates the entire execution of an action?

Answer:

ActionInvocation is the interface that holds the Interceptors and the Action instance. It also includes the sequential firing of the associated interceptor stack.

160: Give an example of several methods included into ActionInvocation interface.

Answer:

a) *addPreResultListener(PreResultListener listener):* registers a PreResultListener to be notified after the Action is executed and before the Result is executed.

b) *getAction():* gets the Action associated with the ActionInvocation

c) *getInvocationContext():* gets the ActionContext associated with the ActionInvocation

d) *getProxy():* gets the ActionProxy holding the ActionInvocation

e) *getResult():* if the ActionInvocation has been executed before and the Result is an instance of ActionChainResult, this method will walk down the chain of ActionChainResults until it finds a non-chain result, which will be returned.

f) *getResultCode():* gets the result code returned from the ActionInvocation

g) *getStack():* retrieves the ValueStack

h) *invoke():* invokes the next step in processing the ActionInvocation.

i) *invokeActionOnly():* invokes only the action (not interceptors or results).

j) *setActionEventListener(ActionEventListener listener):* sets the action event listener to respond to key action events

k) *setResultCode(String resultCode):* sets the result code, possibly overriding the one returned by the action.

161: What does an interceptor do when it fires?

Answer:

When an interceptor is fired, the following steps are performed:

a) Do some preprocessing.

b) Pass control on to successive interceptors, and ultimately the action, by calling invoke(), or divert execution by itself returning a control string.

c) Do some postprocessing.

162: What is a TimerInterceptor?

Answer:

It is one of the interceptors included in the struts-default package; it has the purpose to record the duration of an execution.

163: Give example of Struts Utility interceptors. Briefly describe them.

Answer:

a) TIMER - records the execution time of an action

b) LOGGER - provides a simple logging mechanism that logs an entry statement during preprocessing and an exit statement during postprocessing

164: Give example of Struts Data transfer interceptors. Provide a short description.

Answer:

a) *PARAMS (DEFAULTSTACK):* transfers the request parameters to properties exposed by the ValueStack

b) *STATIC-PARAMS (DEFAULTSTACK) :* moves parameters onto properties exposed on the ValueStack

c) *AUTOWIRING:* provides an integration point for using Spring to manage the application resources.

d) *SERVLET-CONFIG (DEFAULTSTACK) :* provides a clean way of injecting various objects from the Servlet API into the actions.

e) *FILEUPLOAD (DEFAULTSTACK):* transforms the files and metadata from multipart requests into regular request parameters so that they can be set on the action just like normal parameters

165: Which interfaces are available for retrieving various objects related to the servlet environment?

Answer:

a) *ServletContextAware:* sets the ServletContext

b) *ServletRequestAware:* sets the HttpServletRequest

c) *ServletResponseAware:* sets the HttpServletResponse

d) *ParameterAware:* sets a map of the request parameters

e) *RequestAware:* sets a map of the request attributes

f) *SessionAware:* sets a map of the session attributes

g) *ApplicationAware:* sets a map of application scope properties

h) *PrincipalAware:* sets the Principal object (security)

166: Give example of Struts Workflow interceptors. Briefly describe them.

Answer:

a) *WORKFLOW (DEFAULTSTACK) :* makes sure there are not validation errors before allowing the interceptor chain to continue (but it doesn't perform any validation)

b) *VALIDATION (DEFAULTSTACK) :* provides a programmatic validation mechanism

c) *PREPARE (DEFAULTSTACK):* provides a generic entry point for arbitrary workflow processing that somebody might want to add to his/her actions

d) *MODELDRIVEN (DEFAULTSTACK) :* conditionally alters the effective functionality of another interceptor without direct programmatic intervention demonstrates the power of the layered interceptor architecture.

167: Which is the purpose of TOKEN and TOKEN-SESSION interceptors?

Answer:

They can be used as part of a system to prevent duplicate form submissions. These two interceptors both do the same thing, differing only in how richly they handle the duplicate request.

168: How are declared the individual interceptors?

Answer:

Interceptor declarations consist of declaring the interceptors that are available and associating them with the actions for which they should fire. Usually they are declared in struts-default.xml file.

169: How can the interceptors be mapped to specific actions? Provide a simple example.

Answer:

The following code snippet shows how to associate two interceptors with an action:

```
<action name="MyAction" class="org.myactions.MyAction">
  <interceptor-ref name="timer"/>
  <interceptor-ref name="logger"/>
  <result>Success.jsp</result>
</action>
```

170: What happens if an action doesn't declare its own interceptors?

Answer:

It inherits the default interceptor reference of the package.

171: What is the purpose of the following code snippet?

```
<interceptor-ref name="workflow">
   <param name="excludeMethods">input,back,cancel,browse</param>
```

</interceptor-ref>

Answer:

It illustrates a sample of passing parameters into interceptors.

172: How can be created a custom interceptor?

Answer:

By implementing Interceptor interface and overriding its three main methods: destroy(), init() and intercept(ActionInvocation invocation).

173: Why OGNL is considered to be an expression language?

Answer:

Because it provides a simple syntax for binding things like Struts tags to specific Java-side properties, for moving data both into and out of the framework; it actually creates the pathways for data to flow through the framework.

174: Can the ValueStack be defined as a virtual object?

Answer:

No, because it only holds objects which all have properties. All the properties of these objects appear as properties of the ValueStack itself, but the ValueStack isn't actually a classic object.

175: Which is Struts' built-in support for converting between the HTTP native strings and Java types?

Answer:

a) *String* – sometimes a string is just a string.

b) *boolean/Boolean* – true and false strings can be converted to both primitive and object versions of Boolean.

c) *char/Character* – primitive or object.

d) *int/Integer, float/Float, long/Long, double/Double* – primitives or objects.

e) *Date* – string version will be in SHORT format of current Locale (for example, 12/10/97).

f) *array* – each string element must be convertible to the array's type.

g) *List* – populated with Strings by default.

h) *Map* – populated with Strings by default.

176: Which interface must implement Struts' type converters?

Answer:

Due to the fact that type conversion is a part of OGNL, all type converters must implement the ognl.TypeConverter interface.

177: What is the ActionContext?

Answer:

An interface which contains all of the data available to the framework's processing of the request/ including things ranging from application data to session- or application-scoped maps.

178: In which categories can be divided Struts' tags?

Answer:

For organizational purposes, they can be broken into four categories:

a) *data tags* - focus on ways to extract data from the ValueStack and/or set values in the ValueStack

b) *control-flow tags* - offer the tools to conditionally alter the flow of the rendering process

c) *UI tags* - offer the tools with which the user can interact and enter data

d) *miscellaneous tag* - set of tags that don't quite fit into the other categories

179: How does Struts interpret the nonstring attributes passed to tags?

Answer:

All nonstring attributes will be interpreted as OGNL expressions and used to locate the property that'll contain the value to be used in the tag processing.

180: How does Struts interpret the string attributes passed to tags?

Answer:

All string attributes will be taken literally as Strings and used as such in the tag processing.

181: Which is the purpose of the data tags? Which types of data tags does Struts offer?

Answer:

Data tags let you get data out of the ValueStack or place variables and objects onto the ValueStack. There are 5 types of data dags: property, set, push, bean, and action.

182: What is the property tag?

Answer:

The property tag provides a quick, convenient way of writing a property into the rendering HTML. Typically, these properties will be on the ValueStack or on some other object in the ActionContext.

183: What is the push tag?

Answer:

A data tag useful when a lot of work is needed for revolving around a single object. It allows you to push properties onto the ValueStack. It has an only attribute - value, which represents the Object which will be pushed on the stack.

184: What is the advantage of using the bean tag?

Answer:

The bean tag is like a hybrid of the set and push tags. The main advantage of using it is that you don't need to work with an existing object. You can create an instance of an object and either push it onto the ValueStack or set a top-level reference to it in the ActionContext. By default, the object will be pushed onto the ValueStack and will remain there for the duration of the tag.

185: Which is the difference between the action and the include tags?

Answer:

Include tag can reference any servlet resource, while the action tag can include only another Struts action within the same Struts application.

186: Which are the operations on collections supported by OGNL?

Answer:

a) *filtering* - allows you to take a collection of objects and filter them according to a rule

b) *projection* - allows you to transform a collection of objects according to a specific rule

187: What is the select component?

Answer:

The select component is perhaps the most common collection-based UI component. This component is built on the HTML select box, which allows the user to select a value from a list of options. In a Java web application/ it's common to build these lists of options from Collections, Maps, or arrays of data.

188: Which are the most commonly used built-in result types?

Answer:

a) *dispatcher* - used in JSPs or other web application resources such as servlets

b) *redirect* - tells browser to redirect to another URL location (default)

c) *redirectAction* - tells browser to redirect to another Struts action

189: What choices do you have if you need to persist data from the initial request to the resource that's the target of your redirect?

Answer:

There are two choices:

a) The first choice is to persist the data in querystring parameters that are dynamically populated with values from the ValueStack.
b) The second option is to persist data to a session-scoped map (this has a couple of drawbacks: it only works when the secondary resource belongs to the same web application and uses unnecessary the session scope as a data storage)

190: How would you setup a redirect install?

Answer:

The redirect result must be declared and mapped to a logical name. And as with all built-in components, this occurs in the strutsdefault.xml document. The following snippet shows the declaration of this result type from that file:

```
<result-type name="redirect"
class="org.apache.struts2.dispatcher.ServletRedirectResult"/>
<action name="SendUserToSearchEngineAction" class="myActionClass">
```

<result type='redirect'>http://www.google.com</result>
</action>

191: Which are three main components at play in the Struts validation framework?

Answer:

These components are:

a) *the domain data* - represents data to be validated

b) *validation metadata* - the middle component which associates individual data properties with the validators that should be used to verify the correctness of the values in those properties at runtime.

c) *validators* - reusable components that contain the logic for performing some fine-grained act of validation

192: What are the field validators?

Answer:

Field validators are validators that operate on an individual *field. Field = data property.*

193: Which interface(s) need to be implemented in order to create a custom validator?

Answer:

All validators need to implement the Validator or FieldValidator interface. The two interfaces represent field and nonfield types of Validators.

194: What is the purpose of the following code snippet?

```
<?xml version="1.0" encoding="UTF-8"?>
 <validators>
  <validator name="testValidator" class="test.utils.TestValidator"/>
 </validators>
```

Answer:

It is a simple declaration of a custom validator (TestValidator) as an available validator that can be referenced under the logical name testValidator.

195: What is the benefit of using a ModelDriven Action?

Answer:

ModelDriven actions expose domain objects via a getModel() method rather than exposing them directly on a JavaBeans property. The ModelDriven usage benefit is that you can access the properties of the domain model object with top-level OGNL syntax.

196: Which are the locations from which validations are collected when the framework begins its processing?

Answer:

a) SuperClass-validation.xml
b) SuperClass-aliasName-validation.xml
c) Interface-validation.xml
d) Interface-aliasName-validation.xml
e) ActionClass-validation.xml
f) ActionClass-aliasName-validation.xml

197: What is the purpose of TextProvider interface?

Answer:

TextProvider is an interface provided by Struts in order to support internationalization. It exposes an overloaded method - getText(). The many versions of this method have at their heart the retrieval of a message value based on a key. In other words, the TextProvider takes a key and tracks down an associated message text from the ResourceBundles that it knows about.

198: Give an example of defining default bundles.

Answer:

In order to define default bundles, you just need to set the value for the Struts property struts.custom.i18n.resources. Example for defining two resource bundles:

struts.custom.i18n.resources = test.utils.bundle1, test.utils.bundle2

199: Which are the ways to add dynamic values into the message texts?

Answer:

There are two ways to add dynamic values into the message texts. The first method uses embedded OGNL expressions to pull values from the ValueStack or ActionContext. The second method uses the native Java mechanisms for adding parameters to resource bundle message texts.

200: What service provides i18n interceptor?

Answer:

It checks to see whether the request contains a parameter named request_locale. If a request_locale parameter exists in the request, then this value is set on the ActionContext, thus overriding the default locale choice made by the framework.

201: Give example of several of the most common used Struts plug-ins.

Answer:

a) *SiteMesh* - a web page look-and-feel, layout, and navigation framework

b) *Apache Tiles* - a framework that allows developers to build templates that simplify the development of web application user interfaces

c) *JFreeChart* - allows an action to return generated charts and graphs to be included in the web page.

202: What are the Struts framework internal components?

Answer:

At the heart of the framework, Struts has an internal component system that builds and configures the framework. It consists of beans, constants, injection framework and internal extension points.

203: Describe Struts' dynamic method invocation feature.

Answer:

This is a powerful feature that helps out by allowing to remove the method name from the mapping altogether and simply pass the method name at runtime. It is implemented by using two declarative architectures:

a) Wildcard method selection
b) Dynamic workflows

204: How can be Struts used in order to prevent duplicate form submits?

Answer:

There are two ways in which Struts framework can be used in order to prevent duplicate form submits:

a) using the <s:token/> form tag
b) creating exceptions to the token interceptor rule

205: What operations can be performed into struts-plugin.xml file?

Answer:

The file offers handling of the following operations:

a) definition of new packages with results, interceptors, and/or actions
b) overriding framework constants
c) introduction of new extension point implementation classes

206: Which portal servlets does Struts support?

Answer:

The Struts 2 Portlet Plugin supports any portal server that is

JSR168 compliant (for e.g. Apache Jetspeed, Portal, Gridsphere, IBM WebSphere, JBoss-Portal, Pluto)

207: How can be changed 'invalid input error' message for a particular field?

Answer:

The default validators provide default error messages. To override the default message, one must create or edit a global resource bundle and add an entry corresponding to the field. Example:

invalid.fieldvalue.user.phoneNumber = Please enter the phone number in the correct format.

208: How can be integrated Spring with a Struts application?

Answer:

In order to integrate Spring with Struts, Spring should be given a chance to handle the objects that are created by Struts. One way to let Spring do this is to provide a Spring extension of the Struts ObjectFactory, the class that creates each of the objects used in the framework.

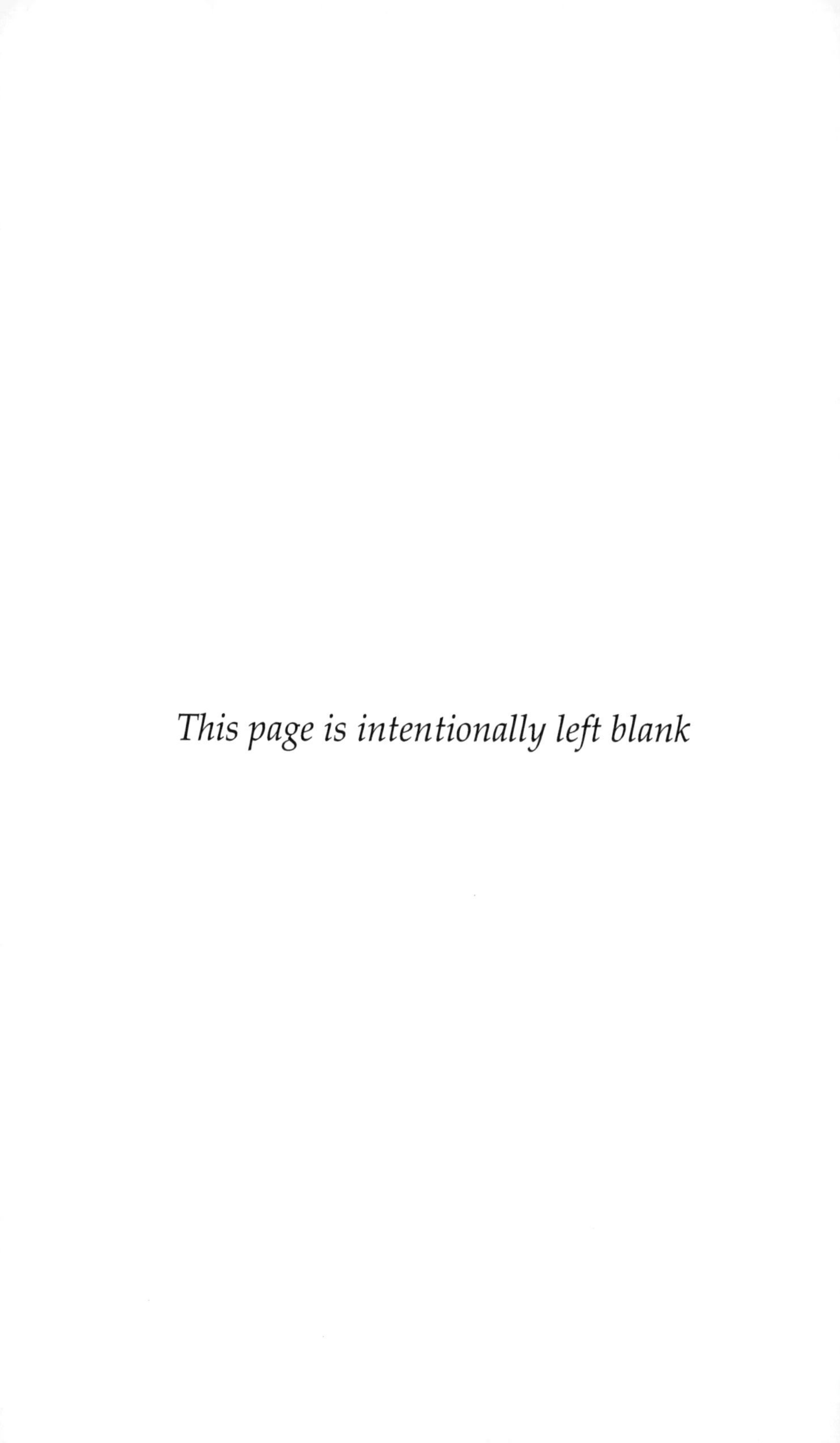

This page is intentionally left blank

HR Questions

Review these typical interview questions and think about how you would answer them. Read the answers listed; you will find best possible answers along with strategies and suggestions.

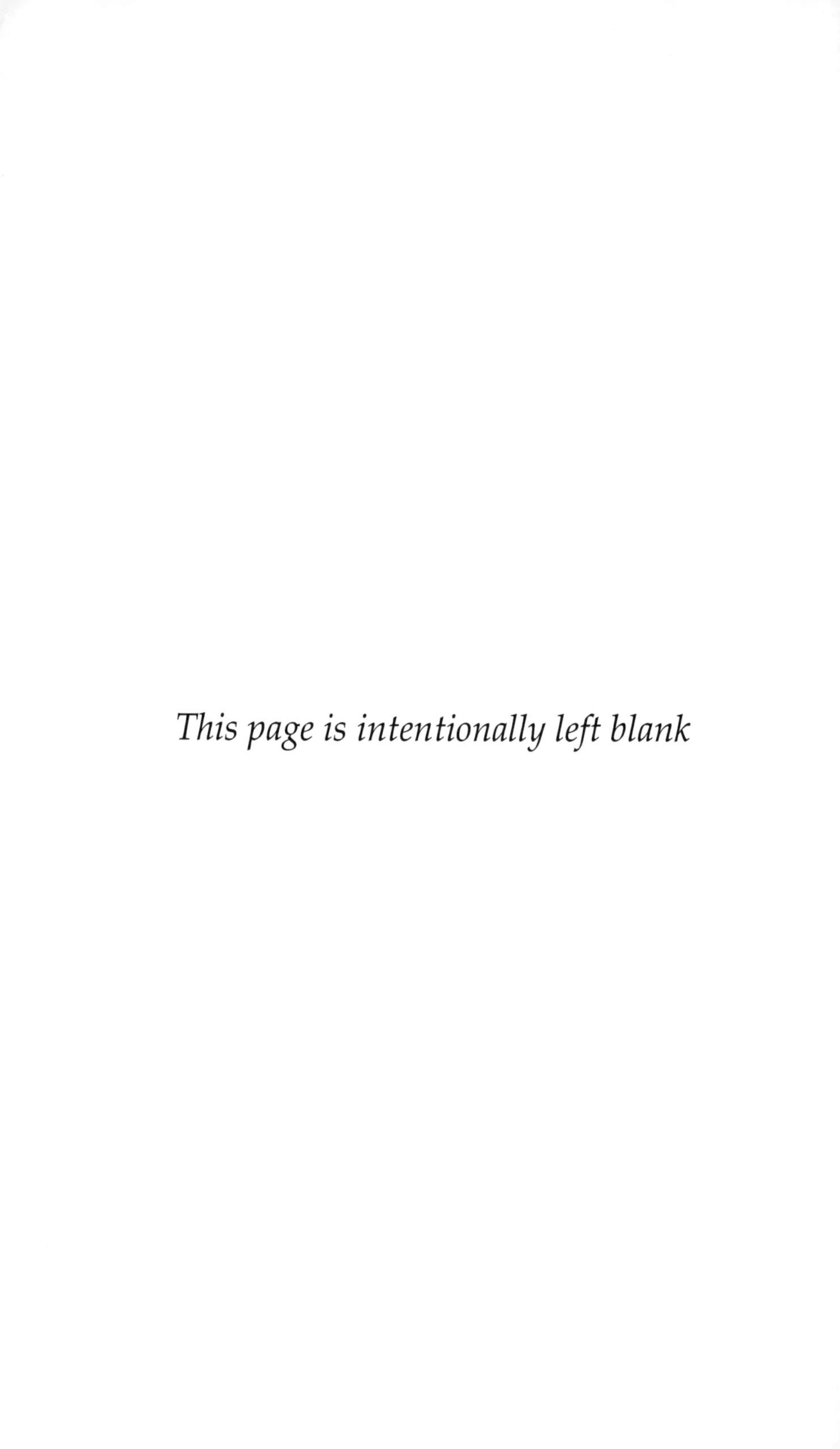

1: Tell me about yourself?

Answer:

The most often asked question in interviews. You need to have a short statement prepared in your mind. Keep your answer to one or two minutes. Don't ramble. Be careful that it does not sound rehearsed. Limit it to work-related items unless instructed otherwise. Talk about things you have done and jobs you have held that relate to the position you are interviewing for. Start with the item farthest back and work up to the present (If you have a profile or personal statement(s) at the top of your CV use this as your starting point).

2: Why did you leave your last job?

Answer:

Stay positive regardless of the circumstances. Never refer to a major problem with management and never speak ill of supervisors, co- workers or the organization. If you do, you will be the one looking bad. Keep smiling and talk about leaving for a positive reason such as an opportunity, a chance to do something special or other forward- looking reasons.

3: What experience do you have in this field?

Answer:

Speak about specifics that relate to the position you are applying for. If you do not have specific experience, get as close as you can.

4: Do you consider yourself successful?

Answer:

You should always answer yes and briefly explain why. A good explanation is that you have set goals, and you have met some and are on track to achieve the others.

5: What do co-workers say about you?

Answer:

Be prepared with a quote or two from co-workers. Either a specific statement or a paraphrase will work. Bill Smith, a co-worker at Clarke Company, always said I was the hardest worker' s he had ever known. It should be as powerful as Bill having said it at the interview herself.

6: What do you know about this organization?

Answer:

This question is one reason to do some research on the organization before the interview. Research the company's products, size, reputation, Image, goals, problems, management style, skills, History and philosophy. Be informed and interested. Find out where they have been and where they are going. What are the current issues and who are the major players?

7: What have you done to improve your knowledge in the last year?

Answer:

Try to include improvement activities that relate to the job. A wide variety of activities can be mentioned as positive self-improvement. Have some good ones handy to mention.

8: Are you applying for other jobs?

Answer:

Be honest but do not spend a lot of time in this area. Keep the focus on this job and what you can do for this organization. Anything else is a distraction.

9: Why do you want to work for this organization?

Answer:

This may take some thought and certainly, should be based on the research you have done on the organization. Sincerity is extremely important here and will easily be sensed. Relate it to your long-term career goals. Never talk about what you want; first talk about their Needs. You want to be part of an exciting forward-moving company. You can make a definite contribution to specific company goals.

10: Do you know anyone who works for us?

Answer:

Be aware of the policy on relatives working for the organization. This can affect your answer even though they asked about friends not relatives. Be careful to mention a friend only if they are well thought of.

11: What kind of salary do you need?

Answer:

A loaded question! A nasty little game that you will probably lose if you answer first. So, do not answer it. Instead, say something like/ that's a tough question. Can you tell me the range for this position? In most cases, the interviewer, taken off guard, will tell you. If not, say that it can depend on the details of the job. Then give a wide range.

12: Are you a team player?

Answer:

You are, of course, a team player. Be sure to have examples ready. Specifics that show you often perform for the good of the team rather than for yourself is good evidence of your team attitude. Do not brag; just say it in a matter-of-fact tone. This is a key point.

13: How long would you expect to work for us if hired?

Answer:

Specifics here are not good. Something like this should work: I'd like it to be a long time. Or As long as we both feel I'm doing a good job.

14: Have you ever had to fire anyone? How did you feel about that?

Answer:

This is serious. Do not make light of it or in any way seem like you like to fire people. At the same time, you will do it when it is the right thing to do. When it comes to the organization versus the individual who has created a harmful situation, you will protect the organization. Remember firing is not the same as layoff or reduction in force.

15: What is your philosophy towards work?

Answer:

The interviewer is not looking for a long or flowery dissertation here. Do you have strong feelings that the job gets done? Yes. That's the type of answer that works best here. Keep it short and positive, showing a benefit to the organization.

16: If you had enough money to retire right now, would you?

Answer:

Answer yes if you would. But since you need to work, this is the type of work you prefer. Do not say yes if you do not mean it.

17: Have you ever been asked to leave a position?

Answer:

If you have not, say no. If you have, be honest, brief and avoid saying negative things about the people or organization involved.

18: Explain how you would be an asset to this organization.

Answer:

You should be anxious for this question. It gives you a chance to highlight your best points as they relate to the position being discussed. Give a little advance thought to this relationship.

19: Why should we hire you?

Answer:

Point out how your assets meet what the organization needs. Also mention about your knowledge, experience, abilities, and skills. Never mention any other candidates to make a comparison.

20: Tell me about a suggestion you have made.

Answer:

Have a good one ready. Be sure and use a suggestion that was accepted and was then considered successful. One related to the type of work applied for is a real plus.

21: What irritates you about co-workers?

Answer:

This is a trap question. Think real hard but fail to come up with anything that irritates you. A short statement that you seem to get along with folks is great.

22: What is your greatest strength?

Answer:

Numerous answers are good, just stay positive. A few good examples: Your ability to prioritize, Your problem-solving skills, Your ability to work under pressure, Your ability to focus on projects, Your professional expertise, Your leadership skills, Your positive attitude

23: Tell me about your dream job or what are you looking for in a job?

Answer:

Stay away from a specific job. You cannot win. If you say the job you are contending for is it, you strain credibility. If you say another job is it, you plant the suspicion that you will be dissatisfied with this position if hired. The best is to stay genetic and say something like: A job where I love the work, like the people, can contribute and can't wait to get to work.

24: Why do you think you would do well at this job?

Answer:

Give several reasons and include skills, experience and interest.

25: What do you find the most attractive about this position? (Least attractive?)

Answer:

a) List a couple of attractive factors such as the responsibility the post offers and the opportunity to work with experienced teams that have a reputation for innovation and creativity.
b) Say you'd need more information and time before being able to make a judgment on any unattractive aspects.

26: What kind of person would you refuse to work with?

Answer:

Do not be trivial. It would take disloyalty to the organization, violence or lawbreaking to get you to object. Minor objections will label you as a whiner.

27: What is more important to you: the money or the work?

Answer:

Money is always important, but the work is the most important. There is no better answer.

28: What would your previous supervisor say your strongest point is?

Answer:

There are numerous good possibilities:

Loyalty, Energy, Positive attitude, Leadership, Team player,

Expertise, Initiative, Patience, Hard work, Creativity, Problem solver.

29: Tell me about a problem you had with a supervisor.

Answer:

Biggest trap of all! This is a test to see if you will speak ill of your boss. If you fall for it and tell about a problem with a former boss, you may well below the interview right there. Stay positive and develop a poor memory about any trouble with a supervisor.

30: What has disappointed you about a job?

Answer:

Don't get trivial or negative. Safe areas are few but can include: Not enough of a challenge. You were laid off in a reduction Company did not win a contract, which would have given you more responsibility.

31: Tell me about your ability to work under pressure.

Answer:

You may say that you thrive under certain types of pressure. Give an example that relates to the type of position applied for.

32: Do your skills match this job or another job more closely?

Answer:

Probably this one! Do not give fuel to the suspicion that you may want another job more than this one.

33: What motivates you to do your best on the job?

Answer:

This is a personal trait that only you can say, but good examples are: Challenge, Achievement, and Recognition.

34: Are you willing to work overtime? Nights? Weekends?

Answer:

This is up to you. Be totally honest.

35: How would you know you were successful on this job?

Answer:

Several ways are good measures:

You set high standards for yourself and meet them. Your outcomes are a success. Your boss tells you that you are successful and doing a great job.

36: Would you be willing to relocate if required?

Answer:

You should be clear on this with your family prior to the interview if you think there is a chance it may come up. Do not say yes just to get the job if the real answer is no. This can create a lot of problems later on in your career. Be honest at this point. This will save you from future grief.

37: Are you willing to put the interests of the organization ahead of your own?

Answer:

This is a straight loyalty and dedication question. Do not worry about the deep ethical and philosophical implications. Just say yes.

38: Describe your management style.

Answer:

Try to avoid labels. Some of the more common labels, like progressive, salesman or consensus, can have several meanings or descriptions depending on which management expert you listen to. The situational style is safe, because it says you will manage according to the situation, instead of one size fits all.

39: What have you learned from mistakes on the job?

Answer:

Here you have to come up with something or you strain credibility. Make it small, well intentioned mistake with a positive lesson learned. An example would be, working too far ahead of colleagues on a project and thus throwing coordination off.

40: Do you have any blind spots?

Answer:

Trick question! If you know about blind spots, they are no longer blind spots. Do not reveal any personal areas of concern here. Let them do their own discovery on your bad points. Do not hand it to them.

41: If you were hiring a person for this job, what would you look for?

Answer:

Be careful to mention traits that are needed and that you have.

42: Do you think you are overqualified for this position?

Answer:

Regardless of your qualifications, state that you are very well qualified for the position you've been interviewed for.

43: How do you propose to compensate for your lack of experience?

Answer:

First, if you have experience that the interviewer does not know about, bring that up: Then, point out (if true) that you are a hard working quick learner.

44: What qualities do you look for in a boss?

Answer:

Be generic and positive. Safe qualities are knowledgeable, a sense of humor, fair, loyal to subordinates and holder of high standards. All bosses think they have these traits.

45: Tell me about a time when you helped resolve a dispute between others.

Answer:

Pick a specific incident. Concentrate on your problem solving technique and not the dispute you settled.

46: What position do you prefer on a team working on a project?

Answer:

Be honest. If you are comfortable in different roles, point that out.

47: Describe your work ethic.

Answer:

Emphasize benefits to the organization. Things like, determination to get the job done and work hard but enjoy your work are good.

48: What has been your biggest professional disappointment?

Answer:

Be sure that you refer to something that was beyond your control. Show acceptance and no negative feelings.

49: Tell me about the most fun you have had on the job.

Answer:

Talk about having fun by accomplishing something for the organization.

50: What would you do for us? (What can you do for us that someone else can't?)

a) Relate past experiences that represent success in Working for your previous employer.

b) Talk about your fresh perspective and the relevant experience you can bring to the company.

c) Highlight your track record of providing creative, Workable solutions.

51: Do you have any questions for me?

Answer:

Always have some questions prepared. Questions prepared where you will be an asset to the organization are good. How soon will I be able to be productive? What type of projects will I be able to assist on?, are few examples.

And Finally Good Luck!

INDEX

Hibernate, Spring & Struts Questions

Hibernate

42: What are the interfaces provided by Hibernate that applications may use when defining custom mapping types?
43: Which Java collections are supported by Hibernate?
44: What is the effect of cascade on inverse?
45: What is a many-valued entity association?
46: What is a polymorphic association?
47: Which operations have Hibernate to handle in order to support portability across different DBMS?
48: Which are the rules that ensure data consistency?
49: What support does Hibernate offer for index creation?
50: What are the transient objects?
51: What is a persistent object?
52: What is the persistence context? Why is it useful?
53: Define the Hibernate conversations concept.
54: What is a business key?
55: Which services provide Hibernate's persistence manager API?
56: Describe Hibernate replication mechanism. Provide a short replication example.
57: What is the purpose/usage of Hibernate ReplicationMode?
58: In which cases do Hibernate flushes occur?
59: Which are the typed exceptions are thrown by Hibernate?
60: Which configuration options must be set in order to enable CMT with Hibernate?
61: Which Hibernate configuration option sets the JDBC connections isolation levels?
62: Which are the LockModes supported by Hibernate?
63: How to implement a conversation that doesn't involve detached objects?
64: What is the transitive persistence?
65: Which is the difference between Hibernate Query Language (HQL)and SQL?
66: In which context is StatelessSession used?
67: Which ways to get objects out of the database does Hibernate provide?
68: Shortly describe Hibernate's cache architecture.
69: Which open source cache providers are built into Hibernate?
70: How can Hibernate be accessed using Spring ?

Spring

71: What is Dependency Injection/Inversion of Control? How is this core concept implemented in Spring framework?
72: Which tools offers Spring framework in order to achieve IoC?
73: What is AOP? What is the difference between AOP and OOP?
74: Which are the core AOP Concepts?
75: What are the main Advice types?
76: Enumerate several methods from BeanFactory interface.
77: Which is the most commonly used simple BeanFactory implementation? Give an example for creating such an object.
78: How can a bean be retrieved from a BeanFactory?
79: What is the relation between BeanFactory and ApplicationContext?
80: How can a bean be identified within ApplicationContext?
81: Which are the most commonly used implementations of ApplicationContext? When should they be used?
82: Which is the difference between uses of FileSystemXmlApplicationContext and ClassPathXmlApplicationContext?
83: Which is the difference between an application context and a bean factory regarding how singleton beans are loaded?
84: Which is the difference regarding lifecycle between a traditional Java bean and a bean within a Spring container?

85: Which is the lifecycle of a bean in Spring context?
86: What does "wiring" mean?
87: Which Spring containers support wiring through XML?
88: Can you recognize the purpose of the following xml file?
89: Which are the methods provided by InitializingBean and DisposableBean interfaces?
90: What is a setter injection?
91: Could you provide an example of setter injection?
92: Does Spring framework offer any alternative to setter injec tion?
93: What is the similarity and difference between setter and constructor injection?
94: What does the following code do?
95: Supposing you have a class Test defined as following:
96: Why constructor injection is used? What will be counter arguments in using it?
97: What is the benefit of autowiring?
98: What are the four types of autowiring?
99: How are pointcuts defined in Spring?
100: Why static pointcuts are preferred over dynamic ones?
101: Which class/method needs to be implemented in order to create a custom static pointcut?
102: Which is the built-in dynamic pointcut offered by Spring?
103: Which class/method needs to be implemented in order to create a cu stom dynamic pointcut?
104: Enumerate several pointcut types supported by Spring framework?
105: How are Introductions implemented in Spring?
106: When would somebody use ProxyFactoryBean objects? Describe several ProxyFactoryBean properties.
107: Which are the two Spring classes that provide autoproxy support?
108: Which is the most common use for metadata autoproxying?
109: What are the advantages of accessing the DAOs through interfaces?
1100 What kind of exceptions does Spring's DAO frameworks throw?
111: Which Spring interface is responsible for mapping a ResultSet row to an object? Give a short example.
1120 Which is the difference between Spring's support for programmatic transaction management and the one offered by EJB?
113: Give example of several Spring transaction managers and their usage.
114: What is a Spring transaction attribute?
115: Which are the RPC models supported by Spring?
116: How does Spring provide support for EJB?
117: Which mechanisms provide Spring in order to access EJBs?
118: Which support classes offers Spring in order to ease the development of EJBs?
119: How does Spring offer JNDI support along with all of the benefits of dependency injection?
120: How does Spring offer e-mail support?
121: What is a MVC front controller? Which is Spring's MVC front controller servlet?
122: Which is the interface implemented by all Spring MVC's handlers?
123: Describe several Spring controller classes and their usage.
124: Define a Spring form controller. What is it used for?
125: What is the interface that accommodates validation for Spring MVC? Describe its main methods.
126: Which class must be extended in order to construct a wizard controller? Which are the compulsory methods of this class?
127: Which is the difference between the wizard controllers and the other command controllers?
128: Give an example of a Spring controller which is able to perform multiple actions.
129: Which is Spring's default method name resolver? Give example of other method name resolvers.
130: How can a view be defined in Spring MVC?
131: Which are Spring implementations of ViewResolver?

132: What is BeanNameViewResolver?
133: Which class supports the creation of PDF files as views in Spring MVC?
134: What is the Spring API used for manipulating PDF documents?
135: What is Acegi Security System?
136: Which is the main mechanism used by Acegi in order to secure we b applications?
137: Which are the mechanisms offered by Acegi in order to authenticate against a database?
138: Which is the difference between DaoAuthenticationProvider and PasswordDaoAuthenticationProvider?
139: What are the password encoders provided by Acegi?
140: Which are the Acegi implementations of CasProxyDecider?

Struts

141: What design pattern does Struts implement?
142: What architectural features are introduced by Struts?
143: What does Struts 2 framework bring in comparison with Struts 1?
144: How are MVC concerns implemented in Struts framework?
145: Which is the role of a Struts action?
146: What are the Struts interceptors?
147: What is the Object-Graph Navigation Language?
148: What is the ValueStack?
149: Which are the mechanisms for declaring the architecture of a Struts application?
150: Which is the purpose of the intelligent defaults?
151: Which are the most important elements in the deployment de scriptor for a Struts application?
152: What does a Struts action do?
153: Which are the constants defined by the Action interface?
154: Give an example of a class that provides default implementations of the Action interface.
155: How does Struts offer su pport for localizing message text?
156: What are the ModelDriven actions?
157: What is the potential danger in using domain objects for data transfer?
158: What does the fileUpload interceptor do?
159: Which is the interface which orchestrates the entire e xecution of an action?
160: Give an example of several methods included into ActionInvocation interface.
161: What does an interceptor do when it fires?
162: What is a TimerInterceptor?
163: Give example of Struts Utility interceptors. Briefly describe th em.
164: Give example of Struts Data transfer interceptors. Provide a short description.
165: Which interfaces are available for retrieving various objects related to the servlet environment?
166: Give example of Struts Workflow interceptors. Briefly descr ibe them.
167: Which is the purpose of TOKEN and TOKEN -SESSION interceptors?
168: How are declared the individual interceptors?
169: How can the interceptors be mapped to specific actions? Provide a simple example.
1700 What happens if an action doesn't declare its own interceptors?
171: What is the purpose of the following code snippet?
172: How can be created a custom interceptor?
173: Why OGNL is considered to be an expression language?
174: Can the ValueStack be defined as a virtual object?
175: Which is Struts' built-in support for converting between the HTTP native strings and Java types?
176: Which interface must implement Struts' type converters?
177: What is the ActionContext?
178: In which categories can be divided Struts' tags?
179: How does Struts interpret the nonstring attributes passed to tags?
180: How does Struts interpret the string attributes passed to tags?

181: Which is the purpose of the data tags? Which types of data tags does Struts offer?
182: What is the property tag?
183: What is the push tag?
184: What is the advantage of using the bean tag?
185: Which is the difference between the action and the include tags?
186: Which are the operations on collections supported by OGNL?
187: What is the select component?
188: Which are the most commonly used built-in result types?
189: What choices do you have if you need to persist data from the initial request to the resource that's the target of your redirect?
190: How would you setup a redirect install?
191: Which are three main components at play in the Struts validation framework?
192: What are the field validators?
193: Which interface(s) need to be implemented in order to create a custom validator?
194: What is the purpose of the following code snippet?
195: What is the benefit of using a ModelDriven Action?
196: Which are the locations from which validations are collected when the framework begins its processing?
197: What is the purpose of TextProvider interface?
198: Give an example of defining default bundles.
199: Which are the ways to add dynamic values into the message texts?
200: What service provides i18n interceptor?
201: Give example of several of the most common used Struts plug -ins.
202: What are the Struts framework internal components?
203: Describe Struts' dynamic method invocation feature.
204: How can be Struts used in order to prevent duplicate form submits?
205: What operations can be performed into struts-plugin.xml file?
206: Which portal servlets does Struts support?
207: How can be changed 'invalid input error' message for a particular field?
208: How can be integrated Spring with a Struts application?

HR Questions

1: Tell me about yourself?
2: Why did you leave your last job?
3: What experience do you have in this field?
4: Do you consider yourself successful?
5: What do co-workers say about you?
6: What do you know about this organization?
7: What have you done to improve your knowledge in the last year?
8: Are you applying for other jobs?
9: Why do you want to work for this organization?
10: Do you know anyone who works for us?
11: What kind of salary do you need?
12: Are you a team player?
13: How long would you expect to work for us if hired?
14: Have you ever had to fire anyone? How did you feel about that?
15: What is your philosophy towards work?
16: If you had enough money to retire right now, would you?
17: Have you ever been asked to leave a position?
18: Explain how you would be an asset to this organization.
19: Why should we hire you?
20: Tell me about a suggestion you have made.
21: What irritates you about co-workers?
22: What is your greatest strength?
23: Tell me about your dream job or what are you looking for in a job?
24: Why do you think you would do well at this job?
25: What do you find the most attractive about this position? (Least attractive ?)
26: What kind of person would you refuse to work with?
27: What is more important to you: the money or the work?
28: What would your previous supervisor say your strongest point is?
29: Tell me about a problem you had with a supervisor.
30: What has disappointed you about a job?
31: Tell me about your ability to work under pressure.
32: Do your skills match this job or another job more closely?
33: What motivates you to do your best on the job?
34: Are you willing to work overtime? Nights? Weekends?
35: How would you know you were successful on this job?
36: Would you be willing to relocate if required?
37: Are you willing to put the interests of the organization ahead of your own?
38: Describe your management style.
39: What have you learned from mistakes on the job?
40: Do you have any blind spots?
41: If you were hiring a person for this job, what would you look for?
42: Do you think you are overqualified for this position?
43: How do you propose to compensate for your lack of experience?
44: What qualities do you look for in a boss?

45: Tell me about a time when you helped resolve a dispute between others.

46: What position do you prefer on a team working on a project?

47: Describe your work ethic.

48: What has been your biggest professional disappointm ent?

49: Tell me about the most fun you have had on the job.

500 What would you do for us? (What can you do for us that someone else can't?)

51: Do you have any questions for me?

Some of the following titles might also be handy:

1. Oracle / PLSQL Interview Questions
2. ASP.NET Interview Questions
3. VB.NET Interview Questions
4. .NET Framework Interview Questions
5. C#.NET Interview Questions
6. OOPS Interview Questions
7. Core Java Interview Questions
8. JSP-Servlet Interview Questions
9. EJB (J2EE) Interview Questions
10. ADO.NET Interview Questions
11. SQL Server Interview Questions
12. C & C++ Interview Questions
13. 200 (HR) Interview Questions
14. JavaScript Interview Questions
15. JAVA/J2EE Interview Questions
16. Oracle DBA Interview Questions
17. XML Interview Questions
18. UNIX Shell Programming Interview Questions
19. PHP Interview Questions
20. J2ME Interview Questions
21. Hardware and Networking Interview Questions
22. Data Structures & Algorithms Interview Questions
23. Oracle E-Business Suite Interview Questions
24. UML Interview Questions
25. HTML, XHTML & CSS Interview Questions
26. JDBC Interview Questions
27. Hibernate, Springs & Struts Interview Questions
28. Linux Interview Questions

For complete list visit

www.vibrantpublishers.com

Made in the USA
Lexington, KY
05 October 2011